C. E. Freeman, A. Sloman

Andria

With Notes and Introductions intended for the higher Forms of Public Schools

C. E. Freeman, A. Sloman

Andria
With Notes and Introductions intended for the higher Forms of Public Schools

ISBN/EAN: 9783337159245

Printed in Europe, USA, Canada, Australia, Japan

Cover: Foto ©Paul-Georg Meister /pixelio.de

More available books at **www.hansebooks.com**

Clarendon Press Series

P. TERENTI

ANDRIA

FREEMAN AND SLOMAN

London

HENRY FROWDE

Oxford University Press Warehouse

Amen Corner, E.C.

Clarendon Press Series

P. TERENTI

ANDRIA

WITH NOTES AND INTRODUCTIONS

INTENDED FOR THE HIGHER FORMS OF PUBLIC SCHOOLS

BY

C. E. FREEMAN, M.A.

ASSISTANT MASTER OF WESTMINSTER

AND THE

REV. A. SLOMAN, M.A.

MASTER OF THE QUEEN'S SCHOLARS OF WESTMINSTER

Oxford

AT THE CLARENDON PRESS

1885

PREFACE.

In the text of this edition we have followed the MSS. rather than the emendations of editors, unless there seemed to be weighty reasons to the contrary. In the absence, however, of A, the testimony of Donatus or other Scholiasts as to readings earlier than those in the Calliopian MSS. has been sometimes accepted, when supported by intrinsic probability.

In a School edition we have thought it better to print the letter v, and to adopt the modernised spelling of the MSS., except in a few cases where the orthography in Terence's time was demonstrably different: e.g. *o* is substituted for *u* after another *u* or *v*; *quor, quoius, quoi, adpulit*, etc., appear for *cur, cuius, cui, appulit*, etc., and *-is* for *-es* in the accusative plural of such words of the third declension as make the genitive plural in *-ium*.

It is hoped that the stage directions, which have been mainly suggested by practical experience at Westminster, may be of real service. As our opportunities of studying this aspect of the Play are unique, we have endeavoured to make this part of the edition as complete as possible.

We have made constant use of the editions of Umpfenbach, Fleckeisen, R. Klotz, A. Spengel, Meissner, and Wagner,— the first two on textual questions only,—and have occasionally referred to those of Bentley, Zeune (containing the commentaries of Donatus), Stallbaum, Parry, and Papillon.

C. E. F.
A. S.

WESTMINSTER,
June, 1885.

CONTENTS.

INTRODUCTION:
    ROMAN COMEDY AND TERENCE .   ix
    PLOT OF ANDRIA   xix
    METRES AND PROSODY OF ANDRIA .   xxi
    CODICES OF TERENCE. . .   xxvi

TEXT OF ANDRIA   1–55

LIST OF METRES OF ANDRIA . . .   57–59

NOTES TO ANDRIA . .   61–122

INDEX TO NOTES . . .   123–128

INTRODUCTION.

ROMAN COMEDY AND TERENCE.

First beginnings of Dramatic Representations at Rome. The natural bent of the Roman character was too serious and too prosaic to favour the growth of a national drama. More than five hundred years had elapsed since the foundation of the city, before a play of any kind was produced on the Roman stage, and even then it was but a rude adaptation by a foreign author of a foreign work.

Fescennine Verses. Yet there had long existed the germs whence a drama might, under other circumstances, have sprung. The unrestrained merriment of the harvest-home at time of vintage found expression, in Latium as in Greece, in extemporised dialogues more or less metrical in character, and much more than less coarse in expression. The lively genius of the Greeks had from such rude beginnings developed a regular Comedy as early as the sixth century B.C. But, among the Romans, although these rustic effusions were at a very early date sufficiently well established to receive a definite name, *Carmina Fescennina*, from Fescennia, a town in Etruria; yet they never rose above gross personalities and outrageous scurrility[1]. When this license was checked by a stringent clause in

---

[1] See Horace, Ep. 2. 1. 145, seqq.:
Fescennina per hunc inventa licentia morem
Versibus alternis opprobria rustica fudit,
Libertasque recurrentes accepta per annos
Lusit amabiliter, donec iam saevus apertam
In rabiem coepit verti iocus, et per honestas

the Laws of the Twelve Tables, the Fescennine verses became merely a generic name for improvised songs, not always very refined, at weddings, triumphs, or other festal occasions.

Saturae. According to Livy 7. 2, the first '*ludi scenici*' were introduced at Rome 361 B.C. to appease the anger of the gods who had sent a pestilence on the city.

It seems certain that about this time a stage was erected in the Circus at the *Ludi Maximi*, and the first three days of the festival were henceforth occupied with recitations, music, and dancing. Performers from Etruria, called *ludiones*, danced to the music of the flute without words or descriptive action; but the strolling minstrels of Latium (*grassatores, spatiatores*) soon took advantage of the stage to recite their chants with appropriate music and gesture. These performances were named from their miscellaneous character **Saturae**[1]. They were composed in the rugged Saturnian metre, with no connected plot, and did not admit of dialogue.

Fabulae Atellanae. A nearer approach to dramatic form was made in the **Fabulae Atellanae**, broad farces with stock characters, e.g. Maccus, Pappus, Bucco, and Dossenus, analogous to the clown, pantaloon, and harlequin of an English pantomime. Each character had its traditional mask, and the pieces were originally played only by amateurs at private theatricals; but when translations from Greek dramas had monopolised the Roman stage, the Atellan farce was adopted

---

Ire domos impune minax. Doluere cruento
Dente lacessiti, fuit intactis quoque cura
Condicione super communi, quin etiam lex
Poenaque lata, malo quae nollet carmine quemquam
Describi: vertere modum formidine fustis
Ad bene dicendum delectandumque redacti.

[1] From *lanx satura*, a dish of mixed food. The later *Saturae* or Miscellanies, with which we are familiar from the works of Horace, Juvenal, and Persius, were introduced by Lucilius, who died 103 B.C. Cf. Hor. Sat. 1. 10.

as an after-piece, like the Satyric drama among the Greeks, and was regularly performed by professional actors. The name *Atellanae*, from Atella, an Oscan town near Capua, gave rise to the erroneous supposition that these farces were performed at Rome in the Oscan dialect; whereas it was only in accordance with Roman custom to give to dramatic performances a local name which could offend no national prejudices. The records of these plays are scanty, but they appear to have presented extravagant caricatures of special classes, trades, or occurrences, and their grotesque situations and lively humour secured them a lasting place in popular favour.

Laws regulating Dramatic Performances. The failure of the Romans to produce a national drama was due not only to their national 'gravity' but also to the rigid censorship of the laws. Any personal lampoon, any ill-advised criticism of public affairs, met with summary chastisement. *Fuste feritor* was the laconic edict of the Twelve Tables: and the magistrates seem to have had plenary power to scourge any actor at any time or place that they deemed fit.

Public opinion at Rome. To legal harshness was added a moral stigma. No Roman citizen could venture to appear on a public stage without losing his character for ever. The composition and performance of plays were handed over entirely to freedmen and slaves, who did not dare to represent Roman life, or introduce Roman topics. Even the rustic raillery and amateur farces of early Rome had to lay their scene in Tuscan Fescennia or Oscan Atella.

Contact with Greek civilisation. Moreover, in addition to a national deficiency of literary instinct, and ignominious legal penalties, a third cause had operated powerfully in checking any development of dramatic originality. For nearly five centuries the Romans had been engaged in a varying, yet almost ceaseless struggle for supremacy, or even for existence. The defeat of Pyrrhus, 274 B. C., and the final conquest of Tarentum and the other cities of Magna Graecia a few years later, left them undisputed masters of the whole peninsula. They were thus brought into close contact with Greek civilisation at the very moment when they had leisure to attend to it. There began at once to arise an ever-increasing demand for a better education for the Roman youth, and for more varied amusements for the Roman populace. The satisfaction of these demands was delayed by the First Punic War, 264-241 B.C.

Livius Andronicus. In the next year Livius Andronicus, a Tarentine captive who received his freedom for educating the sons of Livius Salinator, produced on the Roman stage [1] a drama translated from the Greek. He also translated the Odyssey into Saturnian verse as a school-room text-book, which was still in use in the boyhood of Horace[2]. Thus at Rome the beginnings both of Epic and Dramatic poetry were due not so much to poetical inspiration as to the needs of the school-room and the Circus. As might be expected in work thus done to order, there was little artistic merit. The few fragments which remain seem crude and barbarous, and we may well believe that the books were never again opened when the rod of an Orbilius was no longer dreaded.

Old Athenian Comedy. There could be no doubt as to the school of Attic Comedy to be chosen for imitation. The Old Comedy of Eupolis, Cratinus or Aristophanes, essentially political in its subjects, abounding in topical allusions and trenchant satire of public men and public matters, could not have been reproduced on a Roman stage.

Middle Comedy. Even the poets of the Middle Comedy, who satirised classes rather than individuals or travestied schools

---

[1] *Serus enim Graecis admovit acumina chartis,*
Et post Punica bella quietus quaerere coepit,
Quid Sophocles et Thespis et Aeschylus utile ferrent.
Hor. Ep. 2. 1. 161-163.

[2] *Non equidem insector delendave carmina Livi*
Esse reor, memini quae plagosum mihi parvo
Orbilium dictare.
Hor. Ep. 2. 1. 69-71.

of philosophy, would have seemed far too free to the stern censors of the Republic, and would have been almost unintelligible to the majority of Romans.

New Comedy. The New Comedy was alone available. This was the name given to a school of dramatists, of whom the best known are Philemon, Diphilus, Apollodorus of Carystus, and above all Menander. They wrote at a period (340-260 B.C.) when the power of Macedon had crushed the liberty of Greece. Political life was dead; social life was idle and corrupt. The natural products of such a period of decay were the 'Society' plays of the New Comedy. Their aim was merely to give amusing sketches of every day life[1]. The savage satire of Aristophanes only survived in good-humoured banter. The keen strife of Conservatism against Democracy was replaced by intrigues of amorous youths or crafty slaves to out-wit the head of the family. The interest of these plays was not local but cosmopolitan. Human nature is pretty much the same in all ages, and so these plays were naturally suited for the Roman stage. They were amusing, without the slightest tendency to criticise points of national interest, or otherwise offend against the strict regulations of the Roman magistrates.

Cn. Naevius, 235-204 B.C., the first imitator of Livius Andronicus, a Campanian of great ability and force of character, did indeed dare to write with something of Aristophanic freedom. But his temerity in assailing the haughty Metelli, and even the mighty Africanus himself, led first to imprisonment and afterwards to banishment. The experiment was not repeated.

Plautus and Terence. Between 230 and 160 B.C. the writers of Comedy were fairly numerous[2], but only two have

---

[1] Cf. Cic. Rep. 4. 11, *imitationem vitae, speculum consuetudinis, imaginem veritatis.*

[2] e.g. Caecilius, Licinius, Atilius, and others. Ennius, whose fame rests on his Epic poem, also adapted Greek plays, chiefly tragedies, to the Roman stage.

bequeathed to posterity more than scattered fragments. These two are Titus Maccius Plautus and Publius Terentius Afer.

Life and Works of Terence. Plautus died in 184 B.C. Terence was born in 195 B.C. at Carthage, whence his cognomen 'Afer.' He was a slave, but must early have shown signs of ability for his master Terentius Lucanus gave him a good education, and before long his freedom. His talents gained him admission to the literary clique, known as the Scipionic circle, the fashionable representatives of the new Hellenic culture. Scipio Aemilianus was the centre of the coterie, which included Laelius and Furius Philo, Sulpicius Gallus, Q. Fabius Labeo, M. Popillius, the philosopher Panaetius, and the historian Polybius. These being men of education and taste, unreservedly recognised the immeasurable superiority of Greek literature as compared with the rude efforts of their native writers. To present to a Roman audience a faithful reproduction of the best Hellenic models, in pure and polished Latin, seemed to them the ideal of literary excellence. Style was more valued than strength, correctness of form more than originality of thought. Such was the literary atmosphere which Terence breathed; and his enemies, not confining themselves to gross aspersions on his moral character, openly affirmed that the plays produced under his name were really the work of his distinguished patrons. How far Scipio or Laelius may have had some hand in his plays can never be known, Terence at any rate did not care to refute the report which doubtless flattered his noble friends, but rather prided himself on the intimacy and approbation of so select a circle[1]. All the plays of Terence,

---

[1] *Nam quod isti dicunt malevoli, homines nobilis*
Eum adiutare adsidueque una scribere;
Quod illi maledictum vemens esse existumant,
Eam laudem hic ducit maximam, quom illis placet,
Qui vobis univorsis et populo placent,
Quorum opera in bello, in otio, in negotio
Suo quisque tempore usus't sine superbia.
Adelphi Prol. 15—21.

as of Plautus, were *Comoediae palliatae*, i. e. plays wherein the scene and characters are Greek, as opposed to *Comoediae togatae*, where the scene is laid in Rome or at least in Italy. *Praetextatae* was a name given to historic or tragic plays.

Terence's first comedy, the Andria, was produced 166 B.C. Suetonius relates that when this play was offered to the Aediles, the young author was told to submit it to the judgment of Caecilius. Terence arrived when the veteran poet was at supper, and being in mean attire was seated on a stool near the table. But he had read no more than a few lines, when Caecilius bade him take a place upon his couch, and bestowed high commendation on the play. As Caecilius died in 168 B. C., the Andria must have been in manuscript at least two years before its performance, and some colour is given to the above anecdote by the mention which Terence makes in the Prologue of the ill-natured criticisms of Luscius Lanuvinus. The Hecyra, his second play, proved his least successful one. At its first performance in 165 B. C., the audience deserted the theatre to look at some boxers; a similar fate attended a second representation in 160 B. C., and only the personal intercession of the manager, Ambivius Turpio, secured it a hearing at all. The Hauton Timorumenos appeared in 163, the Eunuchus and Phormio in 161, the Adelphi in 160. In the same year Terence visited Greece, either to study for himself Athenian manners and customs, or, as some assert, to escape the persecution of his enemies. According to one account[1] he perished by shipwreck in 159 B. C., as he was returning to Italy with no less than 108 of Menander's comedies translated into Latin. A more general belief was that he died at Stymphalus, in Arcadia, from grief on hearing of the loss of his MSS., which he had sent on before him by sea. Porcius Licinus narrates that his noble patrons suffered him to die in such abject poverty that he had not even a lodging at Rome whither a slave might have brought news of his death. This is probably untrue, for Suetonius writes that he left gardens

---

[1] Cf. Suetonius, Vita Terenti 4-5.

of twenty jugera in extent on the Appian Way, and his daughter afterwards married a Roman knight.

In personal appearance Terence is said to have been of middle height, with a slight figure and reddish-brown hair. Of his character we know nothing, save what can be gathered from his prologues. These indicate a lack of independence and confidence. He evidently feels that he is not a popular poet. He never professes to be more than an adapter from Greek models; imitation, not creation, was the object of his art.

Contrast of Plautus and Terence. This sensitive protégé of patrician patrons has none of the vigorous personality of Plautus. Indeed, though the literary activity of the two poets is only separated by a single generation, their works belong to different epochs of literature. Plautus wrote for the people, he aimed at the broad effect on the stage, his fun was natural and not unfrequently boisterous. Circumstances forced him to adapt foreign plays and lay his scenes in foreign cities, but he was not careful to disguise his true nationality, and freely introduced Roman names, allusions, and customs wherever they might contribute to the dramatic effect on the heterogeneous audience which crowded to the gratuitous entertainments of a Roman holiday.

Between such plays and the polished productions of Terence there is a world of difference. Terence sought the approbation, not of the uncultured masses, but of a select circle of literary men. His highest aim was to produce in the purest Latin a perfect representation of the comedies of Menander and his school. His cardinal virtues, as a writer, were correctness of language and consistency of character. His scene is always laid at Athens, and not once in his six plays is to be found an allusion which is distinctively Roman. Indeed, the whole tone of his writings was cosmopolitan. Human nature, under the somewhat common-place conditions of every-day life in a civilised community, was his subject; *Homo sum, humani nihil a me alienum puto*, was his motto. His plays breathe a spirit of broad-minded liberality, and their simple unaffected style,

INTRODUCTION. xvii

the easy yet pointed dialogue, the terse and dramatic descriptions, and the admirable delicacy of the pourtrayal of character, won for Terence from the cultured taste of the Augustan age a more favourable verdict[1] than he could have expected from the rude and unlettered masses who most enjoyed the broad fun of a boisterous farce. The above characteristics secured for Terence considerable attention at the Renaissance in Europe. In England several of the minor dramatists are under obligations to him, while in France his influence profoundly affected Molière, and is in no small degree responsible for the long-continued servitude of the French drama to the 'unities' of time and place which have so cramped its free development. The Andria has been adapted to the French stage by Baron as *L'Andrienne*, while Sir Richard Steele has presented it in an English dress as *The Conscious Lovers*.

As might be expected, the characters in Terence, though admirably drawn, are rather commonplace. No personality in his plays stands out in the memory like that of Tyndarus in the *Captivi*, or Stasimus in the *Trinummus*. His morality does not rise above a conventional respectability and a civilised consideration for others, except where the natural impulses inspire a generous disposition with something of nobility.

The discerning criticism of Caesar nearly expresses the more matured judgment of modern times :

---

[1] Afranius writes:

'*Terentio non similem dices quempiam.*'

Cicero writes:

'*Tu quoque, qui solus lecto sermone, Terenti,
Conversum expressumque Latina voce Menandrum
In medium nobis sedatis vocibus effers,
Quidquid come loquens atque omnia dulcia dicens.*'

Horace, Ep. 2. 1. 59, records the general verdict:

*dicitur . . .
Vincere Caecilius gravitate, Terentius arte.*

Volcatius, on the other hand, places Terence below Naevius, Plautus, Caecilius, Licinius, and Atilius.

Tu quoque, tu in summis, O dimidiate Menander,
Poneris et merito, puri sermonis amator.
Lenibus atque utinam scriptis adiuncta foret vis
Comica, ut aequato virtus polleret honore
Cum Graecis, neque in hac despectus parte iaceres;
Unum hoc maceror ac doleo tibi deesse, Terenti.

Not that Terence was devoid of humour; but his humour is so delicate and refined that it must often have fallen flat upon the stage. When his plays are well known their subtle satire and polished wit can be appreciated; but there is without doubt an absence of energy and action (Caesar's *vis comica*), which prevented his pieces from being dramatically successful. An audience must be educated up to his plays before it can perceive their many excellences.

THE EXTANT COMEDIES OF TERENCE.

      ANDRIA.
      HECYRA.
      HAUTON TIMORUMENOS.
      EUNUCHUS.
      PHORMIO.
      ADELPHI.

PLOT OF THE ANDRIA.

The *Andria* takes its name from the Andrian woman, Glycerium, with whose history and fortunes the action of the Play is largely concerned. The familiar characters of the Latin Comedy appear on the stage, the respectable father, the amorous son, and the intriguing slave.

Many years before the time at which the story is supposed to begin, Chremes, an Athenian citizen, having to make a voyage to Asia, left his daughter Pasiphila under the care of his brother Phania. In consequence of a threatened war (936) the latter took Pasiphila with him and followed his brother, but was shipwrecked on the island of Andros (924), and, being in want, made himself the client of an Andrian citizen, who on Phania's death adopted Pasiphila, changed her name to Glycerium, and brought her up with his own daughter Chrysis (810). Presently this man died, and the two girls went to Athens, where Pamphilus, son of Simo, fell in love with Glycerium. This Pamphilus seems to have been considered a model young man; and Simo, without asking his son's consent, had already made arrangements for his marriage with Philumena, another daughter of Chremes, born since the loss of Glycerium. The prospect of this match was marred by an accident. Chrysis died, and, when her body was being burned, Glycerium went dangerously near the fire; Pamphilus rushed forward to save her, and a scene followed, which showed clearly enough how matters stood. Chremes, on hearing what had happened, declared that he would not allow his daughter to marry such a man as Pamphilus.

Act I. Sc. 1. The Play begins with a dialogue, in which Simo informs his freedman Sosia of the early life of Pamphilus, his engagement to Philumena, the discovery of his passion for Glycerium, and the consequent breaking off of the match; he is determined nevertheless to make Pamphilus believe that the marriage between him and Philumena is to take place after all, chiefly in order to see what his son will do.

Act I. Sc. 2, 3. Thus the first scene makes the position of affairs sufficiently clear to the audience. Next Davos appears, anxious to help the son against the father, but afraid of the consequences to himself. Simo threatens him with the severest penalties, if he hinders the marriage with Philumena.

Act I. Sc. 4, 5. Pamphilus enters, complaining bitterly of the heartless conduct of his father, who has just met him, and told him that he is to be married at once. Mysis, Glycerium's maid, overhears his soliloquy, and urges him to be faithful to her mistress.

Act II. Sc. 1, 2. The second act introduces Charinus, who is in love with Philumena, and is reduced to despair, when he hears from his slave Byrria, that she is to marry Pamphilus; but Davos revives the spirits of both the young men, by the discovery that the marriage is not seriously contemplated.

Act II. Sc. 3, 4, 5, 6. Pamphilus, by the advice of Davos, tells his father that he is ready to marry Philumena, feeling confident that he can make this promise without danger, as Chremes will persist in his refusal.

Act III. Sc. 1, 2. At the beginning of the third act a child is born to Pamphilus and Glycerium; but Simo, who prides himself on his acuteness, believes, and is encouraged by Davos to believe, that this is a mere pretence, intended to prevent Chremes from allowing his daughter's marriage.

Act III. Sc. 3, 4, 5, Act IV. Sc. 1. Chremes, knowing nothing about the baby, is persuaded once more to agree to the marriage. Davos is terrified at this fatal blow to his scheme, Pamphilus is enraged against Davos, and Charinus against Pamphilus; but Pamphilus (**Act IV. Sc. 1, 2**) declares that he never meant to give his consent seriously, and Davos promises to find some way out of the difficulty.

Act IV. Sc. 3, 4, Act V. Sc. 1. He hopes to do this by convincing Chremes that the child really has been born; and accordingly he persuades Mysis to lay it before Simo's door, and, in an amusing dialogue, which Chremes is purposely allowed to hear, he makes her tell him that Pamphilus is the father. This piece of information has the desired effect; Chremes declares that the match must be given up.

Act IV. Sc. 5. However, matters cannot come right, unless it is proved that Glycerium is a respectable wife for Pamphilus; and a *deus ex machina* is provided in the person of the Andrian Crito, cousin of Chrysis, who suddenly appears and is introduced into Glycerium's house.

Act V. Sc. 2, 3, 4, 5, 6. Soon afterwards Davos comes out, and tells the old men, on the authority of Crito, that Glycerium is an 'Athenian citizen.' Simo, believing this to be a lie, summarily sends the slave off to prison, and is bitterly reproaching Pamphilus, when Crito comes out of the house, and explains everything satisfactorily. Pamphilus is made happy, but the fortunes of Charinus do not seem to have been very interesting to Terence, unless we can accept the second ending as genuine.

METRES AND PROSODY.

The object of this Introduction is to explain briefly the metres employed by Terence in the Andria, and to clear up such apparent difficulties of Prosody as may remain after the general scheme of the metres is understood.

These metres are Iambic, Trochaic, Bacchiac, Dactylic, and Cretic, which receive their names from being composed of iambi, trochees, etc., as the case may be, or of some other feet, considered to be equivalent; and the lines are further subdivided according to the number of metres which they contain, and according to their complete or incomplete form. In iambic and trochaic lines a series of two feet is called a *metre* (or dipodia), and the name of the line corresponds to the number of these metres; thus an iambic trimeter is an iambic line, containing three metres or six feet; a trochaic tetrameter is a trochaic line, containing four metres or eight feet. In the other lines, however, i. e. bacchiac, dactylic, and cretic, each separate foot is called a metre. Again, some lines have a number of complete feet; these are called acatalectic; while others are called catalectic, because the last foot is incomplete. Thus a trochaic tetrameter catalectic is a trochaic line of four metres or eight feet, wanting the last syllable, and really containing only seven feet and a half.

I. Iambic.

(*a*) **Iambic Tetrameter Acatalectic**, called **Octonarius**, from its eight complete feet. (Common.)

(*b*) **Iambic Tetrameter Catalectic**, called **Septenarius**, from its seven complete feet. (Less common.)

(*c*) **Iambic Trimeter Acatalectic**, or **Senarius**. (Very common; all the plays of Terence begin with it.)

(*d*) **Iambic Dimeter Acatalectic**, or **Quaternarius**. (Used occasionally.)

(*e*) **Iambic Dimeter Catalectic**. (Rare; in 485.)

These lines consist in their pure form of iambi; but the spondee, tribrach, anapaest, and dactyl are admitted in all feet except the last, which must be an iambus, unless, of course, the verse is catalectic. Moreover, as the Tetrameter is regarded as being composed of two verses, with the division after the fourth foot, that foot is usually an iambus; and such words as *ego, tibi, cedo* (cf. 702, 703, 705), are allowed to stand there as if at the end of a senarius.

II. Trochaic.

(*a*) **Trochaic Tetrameter Acatalectic**, or **Octonarius**. (Not common.)

(*b*) **Trochaic Tetrameter Catalectic**, or **Septenarius**. (Very common.)

(*c*) **Trochaic Dimeter Catalectic**. (246, 517.)

INTRODUCTION. xxiii

These lines consist in their pure form of trochees; the spondee, tribrach, anapaest, and dactyl are also admitted. But only the trochee, tribrach, and sometimes dactyl are found in the seventh foot of the Septenarius; and the eighth foot of the Octonarius is always a trochee or spondee. Trochaic, like Iambic Tetrameters, are considered to be divided after the fourth foot. As the Trochaic metre is more quick and lively than the Iambic, it is naturally employed in scenes where feeling and excitement are represented. In any of the metres above mentioned the spondee is occasionally resolved into a Proceleusmatic (⏑⏑⏑⏑). Cf. 46, 134, 261, 610, 691, 737, 745, 759, 779.

III. OTHER METRES.

(*a*) **Bacchiac Tetrameter Acatalectic**, i. e. four complete bacchii (⏑– –). 481–484.

(*b*) **Dactylic Tetrameter Acatalectic**, i. e. four complete dactyls (–⏑⏑). 625.

(*c*) **Cretic Tetrameter Acatalectic**, i. e. four complete cretics (–⏑–). 626–634 and 637.

635 is an irregular line, apparently made up of two trochaic dipodiae catalectic.

The rules of prosody, as commonly taught, must be considerably modified, if we are to understand the scansion of Plautus and Terence. It must always be remembered that the poets of the late days of the Republic and their successors were writing in a literary language, not in the language of everyday life. The quantity of any syllable was regarded as rigidly fixed, just as we might find it marked in a dictionary. In reading the comic poets we find that not merely the word itself, but its relation to other words is important. We have to consider *accent* as well as quantity; for a remarkable instance cf. 760, where we find *manē, cavĕ*. The chief points, which should be noticed, are given below. For the sake of brevity illustrations are taken from the Andria only; but it must be understood that no assertion is made which cannot be supported by citations from Terence.

I. Shortening of syllables usually regarded as long.

1. Shortening of *vowels* naturally long. This takes place with the final vowel of dissyllabic words:—

(*a*) When the first syllable is short and accented; common in the case of imperatives; e. g. 300 *căvĕ*, and so some scan 255 *ăbĭ*. Wagner expresses this in a formula, $\smile - = \smile \smile$.

(*b*) Before a long accented syllable, so that $\smile - \perp = \smile \smile \perp$; e. g. 403 *cavĕ te ĕsse*, 682 *manĕ cŏncrepuit*, 760 *cavĕ quŏquam*.

2. Shortening of *syllables* long by position:—

(*a*) By dropping or slurring final consonants.

m, 91 *enĭm vero*, 503 *certo enĭm scio*.
s, 262 *patrĭs pudor*, 308 *magĭs lubido*, 412 *erŭs me*, 651 *meŭs carnufex*, 673 *satĭs credo*.
r, 261 *amŏr misericordia*, 301 *datŭrne illa*.
t, 396 *dabĭt nemo*.
d, 302, 745 *apŭd forum*, and perhaps 408 *apŭd te ut*.
n, 271 *egŏn propter*, 399 *ităn credis*, 504 *egŏn te*, 749 *satĭn sanus*, 803 *ităn Chrysis*.

So, too, *l*, *x*, and even *nt*. Monosyllables are very commonly shortened, e. g. 42 *ĭd gratum*, 237 *quid ĕst si haec*, 462 *sed hĭc Pamphilus*, 480 *ego ĭn portu*, 708 *ego hănc visam*.

(*b*) By indifference to double consonants, which Terence probably did not write. Thus *ille* is often used as a pyrrhic, and the first syllable of *omnis* is scanned short (694); for *mn* = *nn* in pronunciation. So 378 *ipsus sibi ĕsse*.

(*c*) By weakening consonants of unaccented syllables, when an accented syllable immediately precedes, e. g. 225 *quĭdem hĕrcle*, or immediately follows, e. g. 66 *sine ĭnvĭdia*, 466 *bonum ĭngĕnium*, 614 *quidem ătque id ago*, 830 *ătque in ĭncĕrtas*, 944 *volŭptăti*. The first syllable of *iste* and *ipse* is often short; cf. 174, 645. Note that in 242, 510, 781 *suam, tuam, eam* probably suffer elision of both vowels, though we *may* elide the last only, and scan *ŭxorem, ĕsse,* as already explained.

II. Retention of the quantity of final vowels originally long. This is much less common in Terence than in Plautus. Many instances given by Wagner are not certain. Probably this retention takes place only when it is helped by a pause, e. g. 437 *potin es mi verum dicerē.*

III. Synizesis. Most dissyllabic words, in which no consonant separates the vowels, may be treated as monosyllables ; e. g. 95 *scias,* 843 *meo,* 296 *tuae,* 880 *sui,* 210 *huius,* 93, 210 *eius,* 765 *quoius*; and so *ēōrum, mēōrum,* &c. *grandiūscula* (814) is noticeable, if it is the right reading. *dehinc* and *proin* are always monosyllabic in Terence. In 202 *circuitione* seems to scan as *circitione, cu* apparently being regarded as = *qu.*

Hiatus is admitted :—

(1) When there is a change of speaker, e.g. 616, 665.

(2) When a line is broken by a strong pause, e.g. 345.

(3) When a word is isolated by the sense, e. g. 264 *incertum.*

(4) After the fourth foot of an Iambic or Trochaic Tetrameter.

It is hardly necessary to note that the interjection *O* is not elided before vowels, e. g. 769, 817 ; nor is *em,* cf. 604.

Occasionally a long vowel is shortened instead of being elided, e. g. 191 *quī amant.* Cf. Verg. Ecl. 8. 108 *an quĭ amant.*

CODICES OF TERENCE.

The MSS. of Terence fall into two classes. Class I is before the recension of Calliopius, Class II after it. Class II is arranged in probable order of antiquity.

CLASS I.

Letter of Reference.	Name of Codex.	Place where it is now kept.	Century.	Remarks.
A.	BEMBINUS.	Vatican.	IV or V.	On parchment in uncial characters.

CLASS II.

Letter of Reference.	Name of Codex.	Place where it is now kept.	Century.	Remarks.
D.	VICTORIANUS.	Vatican.	IX or X.	Also known as C. Laurentianus.
P.	PARISINUS.	Paris.	IX or X.	On parchment in small characters.
C.	VATICANUS.	Vatican.	IX or X.	Copied by a German from the same original as P.
F.	AMBROSIANUS.	Milan.	IX or X.	Andria wanting.
B.	BASILICANUS.	Vatican.	X.	A copy of C., except a gap which was filled up from D.
V.	FRAGMENTUM VINDOBONENSE.	Vienna.	X or XI.	Six sheets containing Andria 912–981.
E.	RICCARDIANUS.	Florence.	XI.	Andria 1–39 wanting.
G.	DECURTATUS.	Vatican.	XI or XII.	Much mutilated.

The Bembine is by far the most important, not merely on account of its antiquity, but because it alone has escaped the recension of Calliopius in the seventh century. Codex A was in bad condition, as its owner Cardinal Bembo testified before the end of the fifteenth century, and Andria 1-786 is now entirely wanting.

It bears a note written by Politian (1493 A. D.) to the effect that he never saw so old a Codex. The hands of two correctors can be discerned: one of ancient date, which only appears twice in the Andria, one about the fifteenth century, which changed and added characters in a 'downright shameless fashion.' But, where not thus tampered with, Codex A possesses an authority sufficient to outweigh all the other MSS. taken together. The later MSS. were so much altered by the Calliopian recension that their independent authority is not very great. In all MSS., even in A, the spelling has been much modernised.

The evidence of the MSS. is to some small extent supplemented by quotations of ancient writers and the commentaries of grammarians.

Of these latter, the most important is Aelius Donatus, tutor of St. Jerome, about 350 A. D., and author of a celebrated grammatical treatise which became the common text-book of mediaeval schools. Priscian (480? A. D.), Servius (about 420 A. D.) in his notes on Vergil, and other more obscure scholiasts are of occasional service.

P. TERENTI
ANDRIA.

GRAECA · MENANDRV · ACTA · LVDIS · MEGA-
LENSIBVS · MARCO · FVLVIO · MANIO · GLABRI-
ONE · AED · CVR · EGERE · L · AMBIVIVS · TVRPIO
L · ATILIVS · PRAEN · MODOS · FECIT · FLACCVS
CLAVDI · TIBIIS · PARIB · TOTA · FACTA · PRIMA
M · MARCELLO · C · SVLPICIO · COS

PERSONAE.

SIMO SENEX
SOSIA LIBERTVS
DAVOS SERVOS
MYSIS ANCILLA
PAMPHILVS ADVLESCENS
CHARINVS ADVLESCENS
BYRRIA SERVOS
LESBIA OBSTETRIX
CHREMES SENEX
CRITO HOSPES
DROMO SERVOS.

ANDRIA.

PROLOGVS.

Poéta quom primum ánimum ad scribendum ádpulit,
Id síbi negoti crédidit solúm dari,
Populo út placerent quás fecisset fábulas.
Verum áliter eveníre multo intéllegit:
Nam in prólogis scribúndis operam abútitur,   5
Non qui árgumentum nárret, sed qui málevoli
Veterís poëtae máledictis respóndeat.
Nunc, quám rem vitio dént, quaeso animum advórtite.
Menánder fecit Ándriam et Perínthiam.
Qui utrámvis recte nórit, ambas nóverit: 10
Non íta sunt dissimili árgumento, séd tamen
Dissímili oratióne sunt factae ác stilo.
Quae cónvenere in Ándriam ex Perínthia
Fatétur transtulísse atque usum pró suis.
Id ístí vituperant fáctum atque in eo dísputant   15
Contáminari nón decere fábulas.
Faciúntne intellegéndo, ut nil intéllegant?
Qui quom húnc accusant, Naévium Plautum Énnium
Accúsant, quos hic nóster auctorés habet,
Quorum aémulari exóptat neglegéntiam   20
Potiús quam istorum obscúram diligéntiam.
Dehinc út quiescant pórro moneo et désinant
Male dícere, malefácta ne noscánt sua.
Favéte, adeste aequo ánimo et rem cognóscite,
Vt pérnoscatis, écquid spei sit rélicuom: 25
Posthác quas faciet de íntegro comoédias,
Spectándae an exigéndae sint vobís prius.

ACTVS I.

SC. 1.

SIMO. SOSIA.

(*Athens: a street: on one side the house of Simo, on the other that of Glycerium. The Scene is unchanged throughout the Play.*)

SI. (*To his slaves, who have brought some things from the market.*) Vos ístaec intro auférte: abite. (*Turning to Sosia.*) Sósia,
Adésdum: paucis té volo. SO. (*Carelessly.*) Dictúm puta:
Nempe út curentur récte haec. SI. Immo aliúd. SO. Quid est,   30
Quod tíbi mea ars efficere hoc possit ámplius?
SI. Nil ístac opus est árte ad hanc rem, quám paro,   5
Sed eís, quas semper ín te intellexí sitas,
Fide ét taciturnitáte. SO. Expecto quíd velis.
SI. (*Earnestly.*) Ego póstquam te emi, a párvolo ut sempér tibi   35
Apúd me iusta et clémens fuerit sérvitus,
Scis. féci ex servo ut ésses libertús mihi,   10
Proptérea quod servíbas liberáliter.
Quod hábui summum prétium persolví tibi.
SO. In mémoria habeo. SI. Haud múto factum. SO. Gaúdeo,   40
Si tíbi quid feci aut fácio quod placeát, Simo,
Et íd grátum fuisse advórsum te habeo grátiam.   15

Sed hŏc mĭhi molestumst : nam ístaec commemorátio
Quasi éxprobratióst inmemori bénefici.
Quin tu úno verbo díc, quid est quod mé velis.   45
SI. Ita fáciam. hoc primum in hác re praedicó tibi :
Quas crédis esse has, nón sunt verae núptiae.   20
SO. Quor símulas igitur? SI. Rem ómnem a principio
    aúdies :
Eo pácto et gnati vítam et consilium meum
Cognósces, et quid fácere in hac re té velim.   50
Nam is póstquam excessit éx ephebis, Sósia,
Liberĭŭs vivendi fúit potestas,—nam ántea   25
Qui scíre posses aút ingenium nóscere,
Dum aetás metus magíster prohibebánt? SO. Itast.
SI. quod plérique omnes fáciunt adulescéntuli,   55
Vt ánimum ad aliquod stúdium adiungant, aút equos
Alere aút canes ad vénandum, aut ad phílosophos,   30
Horum ílle nil egrégie praeter cétera
Studébat, et tamen ómnia haec medíocriter.
Gaudébam. SO. (*Sententiously*.) Non iniúria: nam id
    árbitror   60
Adpríme in vita esse útile, ut nequíd nimis.
SI. Sic víta erat : facile ómnes perferre ác pati :   35
Cum quíbus erat quomque úna, eis sese dédere :
Eorum óbsequi studiís; advorsus némini :
Numquám praeponens se íllis : ita facíllume   65
Sine Invídia laudem invénias et amicós pares.
SO. (*Sententiously*.) Sapiénter vitam instítuit : namque hoc
    témpore   40
Obséquium amicos, véritas odiúm parit.
SI. Intérea mùlier quaédam abhinc triénnium
Ex Ándro commigrávit huc vicíniae,   70
Inópia et cognatórum neglegéntia

Coácta, egregia fórma atque aetate íntegra. 45
SO. (*Interrupting.*) Ei, véreor nequid Ándria adportét mali.
SI. Primo haéc pudice vítam parce ac dúriter
Agébat, lana ac téla victum quaéritans. 75
Qui tum íllam amabant, fórte, ita ut fit, fílium 80
Perdúxere illuc, sécum ut una essét, meum. '
Egomét continuo mécum 'certe cáptus est: 55
Habet.' óbservabam máne illorum sérvolos
Veniéntis aut abeúntis: rogitabam 'heús puer,
Dic sódes, quid heri Pámphilus?' 'quid? sýmbolam
Dedít, cenavit.' gaúdebam. item alió die
Quaerébam: comperiébam nil ad Pámphilum 90
Quicquam áttinere. enímvéro spectatúm satis
Putábam et magnum exémplum continéntiae: 65
Nam quí cum ingeniis cónflictatur eíus modi
Neque cómmovetur ánimus in ea ré tamen,
Scias pósse habere iam ípsum suae vitaé modum. 95
Quom id míhi placebat, tum úno ore omnes ómnia
Bona dícere et laudáre fortunás meas, 70
Qui gnátum haberem táli ingenio praéditum.
Quid vérbis opus est? hác fama inpulsús Chremes
Vltro ád me venit, únicam gnatám suam 100
Cum dóte summa fílio uxorem út daret.
Placuít: despondi: hic núptiis dictúst dies. 75
SO. Quid ígitur obstat, quór non fiant? SI. Aúdies.
Ferme ín diebus paúcis, quibus haec ácta sunt,
Chrysís vicina haec móritur. SO. O factúm bene: 105
Beásti: (*Knowingly.*) metui a Chrýside. SI. Ibi tum fílius
Cum illís, qui amabant Chrýsidem, una aderát frequens: 80
Curábat una fúnus: tristis ínterim,
Non númquam conlacrumábat. placuit tum íd mihi.
Sic cógitabam 'hic párvae consuetúdinis 110

Causa húius mortem tám fert familiáriter:
Quid si ípse amasset? quíd mihi hic faciét patri?' 85
Haec égo putabam esse ómnia humani íngeni
Mansuétique animi offícia. quid multís moror?
Egomét quoque eius caúsa in funus pródeo, 115
Nil súspicans etiám mali. SO. (*Alarmed by the last word.*)
    Hem quid ést? SI. Scies.
Effértur. imus. ínterea inter múlieres, 90
Quae ibi áderant, forte unam áspicio adulescéntulam,
Formá SO. Bona fortásse. SI. et voltu, Sósia,
Adeó modesto, adeó venusto, ut níl supra. 120
Quia túm mihi lamentári praeter céteras
Visást, et quia erat fórma praeter céteras 95
Honésta ac liberáli, accedo ad pédisequas,
Quae sít rogo. sorórem esse aiunt Chrýsidis.
Percússit ilico ánimum. attat, hoc íllud est, 125
Hinc íllae lacrumae, haec íllast·misericórdia.
SO. Quam tímeo, quorsum evádas! SI. Funus ínterim 100
Procédit. sequimur: ád sepulcrum vénimus:
In ígnem inpositast: flétur. interea haéc soror,
Quam díxi, ad flammam accéssit inprudéntius, 130
Satïs cúm periclo. (*With strong excitement.*) ibi tum éxani-
    matus Pámphilus
Bene díssimulatum amórem et celatum índicat: 105
Adcúrrit: mediam múlierem compléctitur:
'Mea Glýcerium' inquit 'quíd agis? quor te is pérditum?'
Tum illa, út consuetum fácile amorem cérneres, 135
Reiécit se·in eum fléns quam familiáriter.
SO. Quid aís? SI. Redeo inde irátus atque aegré ferens: 110
Nec sátis ad obiurgándum causae. díceret
'Quid féci? quid·commérui aut peccaví, pater?
Quae sése in ignem inícere voluit, próhibui: 140

Servávi.' honesta orátiost. **SO.** Recté putas:
(*As if stating a valuable truth.*) Nam si íllum obiurges, vítae
    qui auxiJiúm tuḷiṭ,   115
Quid fácias illi, quí dederit damnum aút malum?
SI. Veníl Chremes postrídie ad me clámitans:
Indígnum facinus: cómperisse, Pámphilum   145
Pro uxóre habere hanc péregrinam. ego íllud sédulo
Negáre factum. ille ínstat factum. dénique   120
Ita túm discedo ab íllo, ut qui sẹ fíliam
Negét daturum, **SO.** Nón tu ibi gnatum? **SI.** Ne haéc quidem
Satĭs vémens causa ad óbiurgandum. **SO.** Quí cedo? 150
SI. 'Tute ípse his rebus fínem praescripstí, pater:
Prope adést, quom alieno móre vivendúmst mihi   125
Sine núnc meo me vívere intereá modo.'
SO. Qui igitúr relictus ést obiurgandí locus?
SI. Si própter amorem uxórem nolit dúcere,   155
Ea prímum ab illo animádvortenda iniúriast.
Et núnc id operam do, út per falsas núptias   130
Vera óbiurgandi caúsa sit, si déneget:
Simúl sceleratus Dávos siquid cónsili
Habet, út consumat núnc, quom nil obsínt doli: 160
Quem ego crédo manibus pédibusque obnixe ómnia
Factúrum: magis id ádeo, mihi ut incómmodet,   135
Quam ut óbsequatur gnáto. **SO.** Quaproptér? **SI.** Rogas?
Mala méns, malus animus. quém quidem ego si sénsero..
        (*Shakes his stick as an apodosis.*)
Sed quíd opust verbis? sín eveniat, quód volo,   165
In Pámphilo ut nil sít morae: restát Chremes,
Qui mi éxorandus ést: et spero cónfore.   140
Nunc tuómst officium, has béne ut adsimules núptias:
Pertérrefacias Dávom: observes fílium,

Quid agát, quid cum illo cónsili captét. SO. Sat est: 170
Curábo: eamus núnciam intro. SI. I praé, sequor.
(*Exit Sosia.*)

SC. 2.

SIMO. DAVOS.

SI. Non dúbiumst, quin uxórem nolit fílius:
Ita Dávom modo timére sensi, ubi núptias
Futúras esse audívit. sed ipse exít foras. (*Enter Davos without seeing Simo.*)
DA. Mirábar, hoc si síc abiret: et eri semper lénitas
Verébar quorsum eváderet: 5 176
Qui póstquam audierat nón datum iri fílio uxorém suo,
(*Emphasizing each separate word.*) Númquam quoiquam
nóstrum verbum fécit neque id aegré tulit.
SI. (*Aside.*) Át nunc faciet, néque, ut opinor, síne tuo
magnó malo.
DA. Id vóluit, nos sic nec opinantis dúci falso gaúdio,
Sperántis iam amotó metu, interea óscitantis ópprimi, 10 181
Ne ésset spatium cógitandi ad dísturbandas núptias:
Astúte. SI. (*Aside.*) Carnuféx quae loquitur? DA. (*Seeing Simo.*) Érus est, neque províderam.
SI. Dave. DA. (*Without looking round.*) Hém, quid est?
SI. Ehodum ád me. DA. (*Still without looking round.*) Quid híc volt? SI. Quíd aïs? DA.
Qua de ré? SI. Rogas?
Meum gnátum rumor ést amare. DA. (*Sarcastically.*) Id
pópulus curat scílicet. 185

SI. Hocíne agis an non? DA. Égo vero istuc. SI. (*To himself.*) Séd nunc ea me exquírere, 15
Iníqui patris est: nám quod antehac fécit, nil ad me áttinet.
Dum témpus ad eam rém tulit, sivi ánimum ut explerét suom:
Nunc híc dies aliám vitam adfert, álios mores póstulat.
(*Turning to Davos and speaking sarcastically.*) Dehinc póstulo sive aéquomst te oro, Dáve, ut redeat iam ín viam. 190
DA. Hoc quíd sit? SI. Omnes, quí amant, graviter síbi dari uxorém ferunt. 20
DA. (*Carelessly.*) Ita áiunt. SI. Tum siquís magistrum cépit ad eam˘ rem ínprobum,
Ipsum ánimum aegrotum ad déteriorem pártem plerumque ádplicat.
DA. Non hércle intellegó. SI. Non? hem. DA. (*Sarcastically.*) Non: Dávos sum, non Oédipus.
SI. Nempe érgo aperte vís quae restant mé loqui? DA. Sané quidem. 195
SI. Si sénsero hodie quícquam in his te núptiis 25
Falláciae conári, quo fiánt minus,
Aut vélle in ea re osténdi, quam sis cállidus:
Verbéribus caesum te ín pistrinum, Dáve, dedam usque ád necem,
Ea lége atque omine, út, si te inde exémerim, ego pro té molam. 200
Quid, hŏc íntellextin? án nondum etiam ne hóc quidem? DA. Immo cállide: 30
Ita apérte ipsam rem módo locutus, nîl circuitione úsus es.
SI. (*Passionately.*) Vbivís facilius pássus sim quam in hác re me delúdier.
DA. (*Derisively, pretending to be shocked at the last word.*)

Bona vérba, quaeso. **SI.** Inrídes? nil me fállis, edicó
    tibi,
Ne témere facias: néque tu hoc dices tíbi non praedictúm.
    cave.   (*Exit Simo, gesticulating.*)   205

SC. 3.

DAVOS.

DA. Enímvéro, Dave, níl locist segnítiae neque socór-
    diae,
Quantum íntellexi módo senis senténtiam de núptiis:
Quae sí non astu próvidentur, me aút erum pessúm dabunt.
Nec quíd agam certumst: Pámphilumne adiútem an aus-
    cultém seni.
Si illúm relinquo, eius vítae timeo: sín opitulor, huíus
    minas,   5 210
Quoi vérba dare diffícilest: primum iám de amore hoc
    cómperit:
Me inténsus servat, néquam faciam in núptiis falláciam.
Si sénserit, perii, aút si lubitum fúerit, causam céperit,
Quo iúre quaque iniúria praecípitem in pistrinúm dabit! 214
Audíreque eorumst óperae pretium audáciam:
Nam incéptiost améntium, haud ámantium:
Quídquid peperisset, décreverúnt tóllere:
Et fíngunt quandam intér se nunc falláciam,   15 220
Civem Átticam esse hanc. 'fúit olim quidám senex
Mercátor: navem is frégit apud Andrum ínsulam:
Is óbiit mortem. ibi tum hánc eiectam Chrýsidis
Patrém recepisse órbam, parvam.' fábulae.
Mi quídem hĕrcle ñon fit véri simile: atque ípsis com-
    mentúm placet.   20 225

(*Door of Glycerium's house opens.*) Sed Mýsis ab ea
egréditur. at ego hinc me ád forum.
Convéniam Pamphilúm, ne de hac re páter inprudentem
ópprimat. (*Exit Davos.*)

SC. 4.

MYSIS.

(*Enter Mysis from Glycerium's house. Stopping at the door,
she speaks to Archilis within.*)
Aúdivi, Archilís, iam dudum : Lésbiam adducí iubes.
Sáne pol ílla témulentast múlier et temerária
Néc satís digna, quoí committas prímo partu múlierem: 230
Támen eam adducam? (*After a pause, turning to the audience.*)
ínportunitátem spectate ániculae:
Quía compotrix éius est. di, dáte facultatem óbsecro 5
Huíc pariundi. atque ílli in aliís pótius peccandí locum.
(*Turns and sees Pamphilus coming on.*) Sed quídnam
Pamphilum éxanimatum vídeo? vereor quíd siet.
Oppériar, ut sciám numquid nam haec túrba tristitiae ád-
ferat. 235

SC. 5.

PAMPHILVS. MYSIS.

(*Enter Pamphilus from the forum; Mysis keeps out of his
way at a little distance.*)
PA. (*Passionately.*) Hŏcinést humanum fáctum aut inceptum? hócinest officiúm patris?
MY. (*Aside.*) Quid íllud est? PA. Pro deúm fidem, quid
ĕst, si haéc non contuméliast?

Vxórem decrerát dare sese mi hódie: nonne opórtuit
Praescísse me ante? nónne prius commúnicatum opórtuit?
MY. (*Aside.*) Miserám me, quod verbum aúdio? 5 240
PA. Quíd? Chremes, qui dénegarat sé commissurúm mihi
Gnátam suam uxorem, íd mutavit, quía me inmutatúm videt?
Itane óbstinate operám dat, ut me a Glýcerio miserum ábstrahat?
Quod sí fit, pereo fúnditus.
Ádeon hominem esse ínvenustum aut ínfelicem quémquam,
  ut ego sum! 10 245
Pró deum atque hominúm fidem!
Núllon ego Chremétis pacto adfínitatem effúgere potero?
Quót modis contémptus, spretus! fácta, transacta ómnia. hem,
Répudiatus répetor: quam ob rem? nísi si id est, quod súspicor:
Áliquid monstri alúnt: ea quoniam némini obtrudí potest,
  15 250
Ítur ad me. **MY.** (*Aside.*) Orátio haec me míseram exanimavít metu.
PA. Nam quíd ego dicam dé patre? ah
Tantámne rem tam néglegenter ágere! praeteriéns modo
Mi apúd forum 'uxor tíbi ducendast, Pámphile, hodie' inquít, 'para:
Abí domum.' id mihi vísust dicere 'abí cito ac suspénde te.' 20 255
Óbstipui: censén me verbum pótuisse ullam próloqui?
Aút causam ullam, inéptam saltem fálsam iniquam? obmútui.
Quód si ego rescissem íd priŭs, quid facerém, siquis nunc mé roget:

Áliquid facerem, ut hóc ne facerem. séd nunc quid primum
  éxequar?
Tót me inpediunt cúrac, quae meum ánimum divorsé
  trahunt: 25 260
Amŏr, mísericordia húius, nuptiárum sollicitátio,
Tum pátrĭs pudor, qui mé tam leni pássŭs ĕst animo úsque
  adhuc
Quae meó quomque animo lúbitumst facere. eine égo ut
  advorser? eí mihi.
Incértumst quid agam. **MY.** (*Aside.*) Mísera tim̯eo 'incértum'
  hoc quorsum áccidat.
Sed núnc peropus est, aút hunc cum ipsa aut de flla me
  advorsum húnc loqui. 30 265
Dum in dúbiost animus, paúlo momento húc vel ílluc
  inpéllitur.
PA. (*Hearing Mysis.*) Quis hīc lóquitur? Mysis, sálve. **MY.**
  O salve, Pámphile. **PA.** Quid agít? **MY.** Rogas?
Labórat e dolóre, atque ex hoc mísera sollicitást, diem
Quia ólim in hunc sunt cónstitutae núptiae. tum autem hóc
  timet, 269
Ne déseras se. **PA.** Hem, egone ístuc conarí queam? 35
Egŏn própter me illam décipí miserám sinam,
Quae mĭhi suom animum atque ómnem vitam crédidit,
Quam ego ánimo egrégie cáram pro uxore hábuerim?
Bene ét pudice eius dóctum atque eductúm sin̯am
Coáctum egestate íngenium inmutárier? 40 275
Non fáciam. **MY.** Haud verear, si ín te sit soló situm:
Sed ŭt vím queas ferte. **PA.** Ádeon me ignavóm putas,
Adeón porró ingratum aút inhumanum aút ferum,
Vt néque me consuetúdo neque amor néque pudor
Commóveat neque commóneat, ut servém fidem? 45 280
MY. Vnum hóc scio, esse méritam, ut memor essés sui.

PA. (*With deep pathos.*) Memor éssem? o Mýsis Mýsis, etiam
   núnc mihi
Scripta ílla dicta súnt in animō Chrýsidis
De Glýcerio. iam férme moriens mé vocat:
Accéssi: vos semótae. nos soli: íncipit,　　　　　　50　285
'Mi Pámphile, huius fórmam atque actatém vides:
Nec clám te est, quam illi núnc utraeque inútiles
Et ád pudicitiam ét ăd rem tutandám sient.
Quod égo per hanc te déxtram oro et geniúm tuom,
Per tuám fidem perque húius solitúdinem　　　　　55　290
Te obtéstor, ne abs te hanc ségreges neu déseras.
Si te ín germani frátris dilexí loco,
Sive haéc te solum sémper fecit máxumi,
Seu tíbi morigera fúit in rebus ómnibus,
Te istí virum do, amícum tutorém patrem:　　　　60　295
Bona nóstra haec tibi permítto et tuae mandó fide.'
Hanc mi ín manum dat: mórs continuo ipsam óccupat.
Accépi: acceptam sérvabo. **MY.** Ita speró quidem.
PA. Sed quór tu abis ab ílla? **MY.** Óbstetricem arcésso.
　　　　　　PA. Propera. atque aúdin?
Verbum únum cavĕ de núptiis, ne ad mórbum hoc etiam.
　　MY. Téneo.　　　　　(*Exeunt.*)　65　300

ACTVS II.

SC. 1.

CHARINVS. BYRRIA. PAMPHILVS.

(*Enter Charinus and Byrria in the middle of a conversation.*)
CH. (*In alarm and astonishment.*) Quíd aïs, Byrriá? datŭrne
  illa Pámphilo hodie núptum? BY. (*Carelessly.*)
  Sic est.
CH. Quí scis? BY. Apŭd forúm modo e Davo aúdivi.
  CH. *Ei* miseró mihi.
Vt ánimus in spe atque ín timore usque ántehac attentús fuit,
Ita, póstquam adempta spés est, lassus cúra confectús stupet.
BY. (*Philosophically.*) Quaéso edepol, Charíne, quoniam nón
  potest id fíeri quod vis,   5 305
Íd velis quod póssit. CH. Nil volo áliud nisi Philúmenam.
  BY. Ah,
Quánto satiust te íd dare operam, qui ístum amorem ex
  ánimo amoveas,
Quam íd loqui, quo mágis lubido frústra incendatúr tua.
CH. (*Bitterly.*) Facile ómnes, quom valémus, recta cónsilia
  aegrotís damus.
Tu si híc sis, aliter séntias. BY. (*With indifference.*) Age
  age, út lubet. CH. Sed Pámphilum   10 310
Video. ómnia experíri certumst priŭs quam pereo. BY.
  (*Aside.*) Quíd hic agit?
CH. Ipsum húnc orabo, huic súpplicabo, amórem huic
  narrabó meum:

Credo ínpetrabo, ut áliquot saltem núptiis prodát dies:
Intérea fiet áliquid, spero. **BY.** (*Aside.*) Id 'áliquid' nil est.
    CH. Býrria,
Quid tíbi videtur? ádeon ad eum? **BY.** Quíd ni? si nil
    ínpetres— 15
(*Enter Pamphilus hurriedly, cutting short Byrria's remark.*)
PA. Charínum video. sálve. **CH.** O salve, Pámphile:
Ád te advenio spém salutem cónsilium auxilium éxpetens.
PA. Néque pol consilí locum habeo néque ad auxilium
    cópiam. 20
Séd istuc quid namst? **CH.** Hódie uxorem dúcis? **PA.**
    Aiunt. **CH.** Pámphile,
Si íd facis, hodié postremum mé vides. **PA.** Quid ita?
    CH. Eí mihi,
Véreor dicere: huíc dic quaeso, Býrria. **BY.** Ego dicám.
    PA. Quid est?
BY. Spónsam hic tuam amat. **CH.** Núnc te per amicí-
    tiam et per amorem óbsecro,
Príncipio ut ne dúcas. **PA.** Dabo equidem óperam. **CH.**
    Sed si id nón potest
Aút tibi nuptiae haéc sunt cordi, **PA.** (*With horror.*) Córdi?
    CH. Saltem aliquót dies
Prófer, dum proficíscor aliquo, né videam. **PA.** Audi núnciam.
Égo, Charine, ne útiquam officium líberi esse homínis
    puto, 30
Quom ís nil mereat, póstulare id grátiae adponí sibi.
Núptias effúgere ego istas málo quam tu apíscier.
CH. Réddidisti animúm. **PA.** Nunc siquid pótes aut tu
    aut hic Býrria,
Fácite fingite ínvenite efficite qui detúr tibi:
Égo id agam, mihi quí ne detur. **CH.** Sát habeo. **PA.**
    Davom óptume 35

Vídeo, quoius consílio fretus sum. **CH.** (*To Byrria.*) Át tu hercle haud quicquám mihi,
Nísi ea quae nil ópŭs sunt scire. fúgin hinc? **BY.** Ego vero ác lubens. (*Exit Byrria.*)

SC. 2.

DAVOS. CHARINVS. PAMPHILVS.

(*Enter Davos, exultant, without seeing Pamphilus and Charinus.*)

DA. Dí boni, boní quid porto? séd ubi inveniam Pámphilum,
Vt metum in quo núnc est adimam atque éxpleam animum gaúdio?
CH. (*Apart to Pamphilus.*) Laétus est nescióquid. **PA.** (*Apart to Charinus.*) Nil est: nóndum haec rescivít mala. 340
DA. Quem égo nunc credo, sí iam audierit síbi paratas núptias,
CH. (*Apart.*) Aúdin tu illum? **DA.** tóto me oppido éxanimatum quaérere. 5
Séd ubi quaeram aut quó nunc primum inténdam? **CH.** (*Apart.*) Cessas ádloqui?
DA. Ábeo. **PA.** Dave, adés, resiste. **DA.** Quís homost, qui me . . ? O Pámphile,
Te ípsum quaero. eúge Charine: ambo ópportune: vós volo. (*Stands between the two.*) 345
PA. Dáve, perii. **DA.** Quín tu hoc audi. **PA.** Intérii. **DA.** (*Impatiently.*) Quid timeás scio.
CH. Méa quidem hercle cérte in dubio vítast. **DA.** Et quid tú, scio. 10

PA. Núptiae mi ... DA. Etsí scio? PA. hodie ... DA.
(*Putting his hands to his ears.*) Obtúndis, tametsi.
intéllego?
(*To Pamphilus.*) Íd paves, ne dúcas tu illam: (*To
Charinus.*) tu aútem, ut ducas. CH. Rém tenes.
PA. Ístuc ipsum. DA. Atqui ístuc ipsum níl periclist:
mé vide. 350
PA. Óbsecro te, quám primum hoc me líbera miserúm
metu. DA. Hem,
Líbero; uxorém tibi non dat iám Chremes. PA. Qui
scís? DA. Scio. 15
Túŏs pater modo mé prehendit: aít tibi uxorém dare
Hódie, item alia múlta, quae nunc nón est narrandí locus.
Cóntinuo ad te próperans percurro ád forum, ut dicám
tibi haec. 355
Vbi te non invénio, ibi ascendo ín quendam excelsúm locum.
Círcumspicio; núsquam. forte ibi húius video Býrriam; 20
Rógŏ: negat vidísse. mihi moléstum. quid agam cógito.
Rédeunti interea éx ipsa re mi íncidit suspítio ' hem,
Paúlulum obsoni: ípsus tristis: de ínproviso núptiae: 360
Nón cohaerent.' PA. Quórsum nam istuc? DA. Égo me
continuo ád Chremem.
Quom illo advenio, sólitudo ante óstium: iam id gaúdeo. 25
CH. Récte dicis. PA. Pérge. DA. Maneo: intérea intro
ire néminem
Vídeo, exire néminem: matrónam nullam in aédibus,
Níl ornati, níl tumulti: accéssi: intro aspexí. PA. Scio:
Mágnum signum. DA. Núm videntur cónvenire haec
núptiis? 366
PA. Nón opinor, Dáve. DA. 'Opinor' nárras? non recte
áccipis. 30

Cérta res est. étiam puerum inde ábiens conveni Chremi:
Hólera et pisciculós minutos férre obolo in cenám seni.
CH. Líberatus sum hódie, Dave, túa opera. DA. Ac nullús quidem. 370
CH. Quíd ita? nempe huic prórsus illam nón dat. DA. Ridiculúm caput,
Quási necess*us* sít, si huic non dat, té illam uxorem dúcere:
Nísi vides, nisi sénis amicos óras, ambis. CH. Béne mones:
Íbo, etsi hercle saépe iam me spés haec frustratást. vale.
       (*Exit Charinus.*)

SC. 3.

PAMPHILVS. DAVOS.

PA. Quíd igitur sibi vólt pater? quor símulat? DA. Ego dicám tibi. 375
Si íd suscenseát nunc, quia non dét tibi uxorém Chremes,
Priús quam tuom ut sese hábeat animum ad núptias perspéxerit:
Ípsus sibi ésse iniúrius videátur, neque id iniúria.
Séd si tu negáris ducere, íbi culpam in te tránsferet: 5
Tum íllae turbae fíent. PA. Quidvis pátiar. DA. Pater est, Pámphile. 380
Difficilest. tum haec sólast mulier. díctum ac factum invénerit
Áliquam causam, quam ób rem eïciat óppido. PA. (*With horror.*) Eïciát? DA. Cito.
PA. Cédo igitur quid fáciam, Dave? DA. Díc te ducturum. PA. Hém. DA. Quid est?

PA. Egŏn dícam? DA. Quor non? PA. Númquam faciam.
　　DA. Né nega.　　　　　　　　　　　　　　　10
PA. Suadére noli. DA. Ex eá re quid fiát, vide.　385
PA. Vt ab ílla excludar (*Pointing to Glycerium's house*), húc
　　concludar. (*Pointing in the opposite direction.*) DA.
　　Nón itast.

Nempe hóc sic esse opínor: dicturúm patrem
'Ducás volo hodie uxórem': tu 'ducam' ínquies:
Cedo quíd iurgabit técum? hic reddes ómnia,　　　15
Quae núnc sunt certa ei cónsilia, incerta út sient,　390
Sine ŏmní periclo: nam hóc haud dubiumst, quín Chremes
Tibi nón det gnatam. néc tu ea causa mínueris
Haec quaé facis, ne is mútet suam senténtiam.
Patrí dic velle: ut, quóm velit, tibi iúre irasci nón queat. 20
Nam quód tu speres, 'própulsabo fácile uxorem his móri-
　　bus:　　　　　　　　　　　　　　　　　　395
Dabĭt némo': inveniet ínopem potius, quám te corrumpí
　　sinat.
Sed sí te aequo animo férre accipiet, néglegentem féceris:
Aliam ótiosus quaéret: interea áliquid acciderít boni.
PA. Ităn crédis? DA. Haud dubium íd quidemst. PA.
　　Vidĕ quó me inducas. DA. Quín taces.　　25
PA. Dicám. puerum autem né resciscat mi ésse ex illa
　　caútiost:　　　　　　　　　　　　　　　400
Nam póllicitus sum súscepturum. DA. O fácinus audax.
　　PA. Hánc fidem
Sibi me óbsecravit, quí se sciret nón deserturum, út darem.
DA. Curábitur. (*The door of Simo's house opens.*)　sed
　　páter adest. cavĕ te ésse tristem séntiat.

SC. 4.

SIMO. DAVOS. PAMPHILVS.

(*Enter Simo, without seeing Davos and Pamphilus.*)
SI. Revíso quid agant aút quid captent cónsili.
DA. (*Apart to Pamphilus.*) Hic núnc non dubitat, quín
        te ducturúm neges.   405
Venít meditatus álicunde ex soló loco:
Orátionem spérat invenísse se,
Qui differat te: proín tu fac apud te út sies.   5
PA. (*Apart to Davos.*) Modo ŭt póssim, Dave. DA.
        (*Apart.*) Créde inquam hoc mihi, Pámphile,
Numquam hódie tecum cómmutaturúm patrem   410
Vnum ésse verbum, sí te dices dúcere.

SC. 5.

BYRRIA. SIMO. DAVOS. PAMPHILVS.

(*Enter Byrria, who remains in the background, unseen by the rest.*)
BY. (*Aside.*) Erŭs mé relictis rébus iussit Pámphilum
Hodie óbservare, ut quíd ageret de núptiis
Scirem: íd propterea núnc hunc venientém sequor.
Ipsum ádeo praesto vídeo cum Davo: hóc agam.   415
SI. (*Aside.*) Vtrúmque adesse vídeo. DA. (*Apart to Pam-
        philus.*) Hem, serva. SI. Pámphile.   5
DA. (*Apart.*) Quasi de ínproviso réspice ad eum. PA.
        Ehém pater.
DA. (*Apart.*) Probe. SI. Hódie uxorem dúcas, ut dixí.
        volo.

BY. (*Aside.*) Nunc nóstrae timeo párti, quid híc respóndeat.
PA. Neque ístíc neque alibi tíbi erit usquam in mé mora.
    BY. (*Aside, alarmed.*) Hem.   420
DA. (*Apart.*) Obmútuit. **BY.** (*Aside.*) Quid díxit? **SI.**
    Facis ut té decet,   10
Quom istúc quod postulo ínpetro cum grátia.
DA. (*Apart.*) Sum vérus? **BY.** (*Aside.*) erus, quantum
    aúdio, uxore éxcidit.
SI. I núnciam intro, ne ín mora, quom opŭs sít, sies.
PA. Eó. (*Exit into Simo's house.*) **BY.** (*Aside.*) Nullane
    in re ésse quoiquam hominí fidem!   425
Verum íllud verbumst, vólgo quod dicí solet,   15
Omnís sibi malle mélius esse quam álteri.
Ego íllam vidi, vírginem formá bona
Meminí videre, quo aéquior sum Támphilo.
Renúntiabo, ut pro hóc malo mihi dét malum.   431
        (*Exit Byrria.*)

SC. 6.

SIMO. DAVOS.

DA. (*Aside.*) Hic núnc me credit áliquam sibi falláciam
Portáre et ea me hic réstitisse grátia.
SI. (*With affected politeness.*) Quid Dávos narrat? **DA.** Aéque
    quicquam núnc quidem.
SI. Nilne? hém. **DA.** Nil prorsus. **SI.** Átqui expecta-
    bám quidem.   435
DA. (*Aside.*) Praetér spem evenit: séntio: hoc male habét
    virum.   5
SI. Potin és mihi verum dícerĕ? **DA.** Nil fácilius.

SI. Num illí molestae quídpiam haec sunt núptiae
Huiúsce propter cónsuetudinem hóspitae?
DA. Nil hércle: aut, si adeo, bíduist aut trídui 440
Haec sóllicitudo: nósti? deinde désinet. 10
Etenim ípsus secum eám rem reputavít via.
SI. Laudó. **DA.** Dum licitumst éï dumque aetás tulit,
Amávit: tum id clam: cávit, ne umquam infámiae
Ea rés sibi esset, út virum fortém decet: 445
Nunc úxore opus est: ánimum ad uxorem ádpulit. 15
SI. Subtrístis visus ést esse aliquantúm mihi.
DA. Nil própter hanc rem, séd ĕst quod suscensét tibi.
SI. Quid námst? **DA.** Puerilest. **SI.** Quíd *id* est. **DA.**
      Nil. **SI.** Quin díc, quid est?
DA. Ait nímium parce fácere sumptum. **SI.** Méne? **DA.** Te.
'Vix' ínquit 'drach*u*mis ést obsonatúm decem: 20 451
Num fílio vidétur uxorém dare?
Quem' inquít 'vocabo ad cénam meorum aequálium
Potíssumum nunc?' ét, quod dicendum híc siet,
Tu quóque per parce nímium. non laudó. **SI.** Tace.
DA. (*Aside.*) Commóvi. **SI.** ego istaec récte ut fiant
      vídero. 25 456
(*Aside.*) Quidnam hóc est rei? quid híc volt veteratór
      sibi?
Nam si híc malist quicquam, hém illic est huic reí caput.

ACTVS III.

SC. 1.

MYSIS. SIMO. DAVOS. LESBIA. GLYCERIVM.

(*Enter Mysis and Lesbia, without seeing Simo and Davos.*)

MY. Ita pól quidem res ést, ut dixti, Lésbia:
Fidélem haud ferme múlieri inveniás virum.   460
SI. (*Apart to Davos.*) Ab Ándriast ancílla haec. DA. (*Apart to Simo.*) Quid narrás? SI. (*Apart.*) Itast.
MY. Sed híc Pámphilus. SI. (*Apart.*) Quid dícit? MY. firmavít fidem. SI. (*Apart.*) Hem.
DA. (*Aside.*) Vtinam aút hic surdus aút haec muta fácta sit.   5
MY. Nam quód peperisset, iússit tolli. SI. (*Apart.*) O Iúppiter,
Quid ego aúdio? actumst, síquidem haec vera praédicat.   465
LE. Bonum íngénium narras ádulescentis. MY. Óptumum.
Sed séquere me intro, ne ín mora illi sís. LE. Sequor.
(*Exeunt Mysis and Lesbia into Glycerium's house.*)
DA. (*Aside.*) Quod rémedium nunc huíc malo inveniám?
SI. Quid hoc?   10
Adeón est demens? éx peregrina? iám scio: ah
Vix tándem sensi stólidus. DA. (*Aside with great sarcasm.*)
Quid híc sensísse ait?   470
SI. (*Aside.*) Haec prímum adfertur iám mi ab hoc fallácia:

Hanc símulant parere, quó Chremetem abstérreant.
   (*Listening to voices suddenly heard in Glycerium's house.*)
(*Turning to Davos.*) Hui, tám cito? ridículum: postquam
   ante óstium
Me audívit stare, adpróperat. non sat cómmode   475
Divísa sunt tempóribus tibi, Dave, haéc. **DA.** Mihin?
SI. Num inmémores discipuli? **DA.** Égo quid narres
   néscio.
SI. (*Aside.*) Hic ínparatum mé si in veris núptiis   20
Adórtus esset, quós mihi ludos rédderet?
Nunc huíus periclo fít, ego in portu návigo.   480

SC. 2.

LESBIA. SIMO. DAVOS.

(*Lesbia, coming out of Glycerium's house, speaks through the
   door to Archilis, who is within. Simo and Davos are at
   the back of the stage.*)
LE. Adhúc, Archilís, quae adsolént quaeque opórtet
Signa ésse ad salútem, omnia huíc esse vídeo.
Nunc prímum fac ísta ut lavét: post deïnde,
Quod iússi ei darí bibere et quántum inperávi,
Date: móx ego huc revórtar.   5 485
(*Turning to the audience.*) Per ecástor scitus púer est natus
   Pámphilo.
Deos quaéso ut sit supérstes, quandoquidem ípsest in-
   genió bono,
Quomque huíc est veritus óptumae adulescénti facere in-
   iúriam.   (*Exit Lesbia.*)

SI. (*Angrily.*) Vel hŏc quís non credat, quí te norit, ábs
   te esse ortum? DA. (*With affected astonishment.*)
   Quíd nam id est?
SI. Non ínperabat córam, quid opus fácto esset puér-
   perae: 10 490
Sed póstquam egressast, íllis quae sunt íntus clamat dé via.
O Dáve, itan contémnor abs te? aut ítane tandem idóneus
Tibi vídeor esse, quém tam aperte fállere incipiás dolis?
Saltem áccurate, ut métui videar cérte, si rescíverim.
DA. (*Aside.*) Certe hércle nunc hic se ípsus fallit, haúd
   ego. SI. Edixín tibi,   15 495
Intérminatus súm, ne faceres: núm veritu's? quid rétulit?
Credón tibi hoc nunc, péperisse hanc e Pámphilo?
DA. (*Aside.*) Teneó quid erret, ét quid agam habeo. SI.
   Quíd taces?
DA. Quid crédas? quasi non tíbi renuntiáta sint haec síc
   fore.
SI. Mihin quísquam? DA. (*Ironically.*) Eho an tute íntel-
   lexti hoc ádsimulari? SI. Inrídeor.   20 500
DA. Renúntiatumst: nám qui istaec tibi íncidit suspítio?
SI. Qui? quía te noram. DA. Quási tu dicas, fáctum
   id consilió meo.
SI. Certe énim scio. DA. (*With an air of injured innocence.*)
   Non sátis me pernosti étiam, qualis sím, Simo.
SI. Egŏn té? DA. Sed siquid tíbi narrare occépi, con-
   tinuó dari
Tibi vérba censes . . . SI. Fálso? DA. Itaque hercle
   níl iam muttire aúdeo.   25 505
SI. Hoc égo scio unum, néminem peperísse hic. DA.
   Intelléxti.
Sed nílo setiús *mox* puerum huc déferent ante óstium.
Id égo iam nunc tibi, ére, renuntió futurum, ut sís sciens,

Ne tu hóc posterius dícas Davi fáctum consilio aút dolis:
Prórsus a me opíniónem hanc tuam ésse ego amotám
    volo.   30   510
SI. (*Incredulously.*) Vnde id scis? DA. Audívi et credo:
    (*Confidentially.*) múlta concurrúnt simul,
Quí coniecturam hánc nunc facio. iám primum postquám
    videt
Núptias domi ádparari, míssast ancilla ílico
Óbstetricem arcéssitum ad eam et púerum ut adferrét
    simul.   35   515
Hóc nisi fit, puerum út tu videas, níl moventur núptiae.
SI. Quíd aïs? quom intelléxeras
Íd consilium cápere, quor non díxti extemplo Pámphilo?
DA. Quís igitur eum ab ílla abstraxit nísi ego? nam om-
    nes nós quidem
Scímus, quam misere hánc amarit. núnc sibi uxorem éx-
    petit.   40   520
Póstremo id mihi dá negoti: tú tamen idem has núptias
Pérge facere ita út facis : et id spéro adiuturós deos.
SI. Ímmo abi intro : ibi me ópperire et quód parato opus
    ést para.   (*Exit Davos into Simo's house.*)
Non ínpulit me, haec núnc omnino ut créderem.
Atque haúd scio an quae díxit sint vera ómnia,   45   525
Sed párvi pendo: illúd mihi multo máxumumst,
Quod míhi pollicitust ípsus gnatus. núnc Chremem
Convéniam: orabo gnáto uxorem : si ínpetro,
Quid álias malim quam hódie has fieri núptias?
Nam gnátus quod pollícitust, haud dubiúmst mihi, 50   530
Si nólit, quin cum mérito possim cógere.
Atque ádeo in ipso témpore eccum ipsum óbviam.

SC. 3.

SIMO. CHREMES.

(*Chremes comes on from the Forum.*)

SI. Iubeó Chremetem ... CH. (*Bluntly interrupting.*)
    O te ípsum quaerebam. SI. Ét ego te. CH.
    Optato ádvenis.
Aliquót me adierunt, éx te auditum qui aíbant, hodie fíliam
Meam núbere tuo gnáto : id viso tún an illi insániant.   535
SI. Auscúlta paucis : ét quid te ego velim ét tu quod
    quaerís scies.
CH. (*Carelessly.*) Auscúlto : loquere quíd velis.   5
SI. (*Earnestly.*) Per té deos oro et nóstram amicitiám,
    Chreme,
Quae incépta a parvis cum aétate adcrevít simul,
Perque únicam gnatám tuam et gnatúm meum,   540
Quoius tíbi potestas súmma servandí datur,
Vt me ádiuves in hác re, atque ita uti núptiae   10
Fueránt futurae, fíant. CH. Ah, ne me óbsecra :
Quasi hóc te orando a me ínpetrare opórteat.
Alium ésse censes núnc me atque olim quóm dabam?   545
Si in rémst utrique ut fíant, arcessí iube.
Sed si éx ea re plús malist quam cómmodi   15
Vtríque, id oro te ín commune ut cónsulas,
Quasi ílla tua sit Pámphilique ego sím pater.
SI. Immo íta volo itaque póstulo ut fiát, Chreme :   550
Neque póstulem abs te, ni ípsa res moneát. CH. Quid est?
SI. Iraé sunt inter Glýcerium et gnatum. CH. (*Care-*
    lessly.) Aúdio.   20
SI. Ita mágnae, ut sperem pósse avelli. CH. (*Impatiently.*)
    Fábulae.

SI. Profécto sic est.   **CH.** Síc hercle ut dicám tibi:
Amántium irae amóris integrátiost.   555
SI. Hem, id te óro ut ante cámus. dum tempús datur,
Dumque eíus lubido occlúsast contuméliis,   25
Priŭs quam hárum scelera et lácrumae confictaé dolis
Reddúcunt animum aegrótum ad misericórdiam,
Vxórem demus. spéro consuetúdine et   560
Coniúgio liberáli devinctúm, Chreme,
Dein fácile ex illis sése emersurúm malis.   30
CH. Tibi ita hóc videtur: át ego non posse árbitror
Neque ĭllum hánc perpetuo habére neque me pérpeti.
SI. Qui scís ergo istuc, nísi periclum féceris?   565
CH. At ĭstúc periclum in fília fierí gravest.
SI. Nempe íncommoditas dénique huc omnís redit,   35
Si evéniat, quod di próhibeant, discéssio.
At sí corrigitur, quót commoditatés vide:
Princípio amico fílium restítueris,   570
Tibi génerum firmum et fíliae inveniés virum.
CH. (*Yielding against his better judgment.*) Quid ĭstíc? si ita
    istuc ánimum induxti esse útile,   40
Noló tibi ullum cómmodum in me claúdier.
SI. Meritó te semper máxumi fecí, Chreme.
CH. Sed quíd aïs?   **SI.** Quid?   **CH.** Qui scís eos nunc
    díscordare intér se?   575
SI. Ipsús mihi Davos, qui íntumust eorúm consiliis, díxit:
Et ís mihi suadet núptias quantúm queam ut matúrem.   45
Num cénses faceret, fílium nisi scíret eadem haec vélle?
Tute ádeo iam eius verba aúdies. (*Calling into his house.*)
    heus, evocate huc Dávom.
Atque éccum: video ipsúm foras exíre.

SC. 4.

DAVOS. SIMO. CHREMES.

(*Davos comes hastily out of Simo's house.*)

DA. Ad te ibam. **SI.** Quíd namst?
DA. (*With pretended anxiety.*) Quor úxor non arcéssitur?
iam advésperascit. **SI.** (*Apart to Chremes.*)
Aúdin? 581
(*Aloud to Davos.*) Ego dúdum non nil véritus sum, Dave,
ábs te, ne faceres idem,
Quod vólgus servorúm solet, dolís ut me delúderes,
Proptérea quod amat fílius. **DA.** Egon ístuc facerem? **SI.**
Crédidi: 5
Idque ádeo metuens vós celavi, quód nunc dicam. **DA.**
Quíd? **SI.** Scies: 585
Nam própemodum habeo iám fidem. **DA.** Tandém cognosti quí siem?
SI. Non fúerant nuptiaé futurae. **DA.** (*With feigned astonishment.*) Quíd? non? **SI.** Sed ea grátia
Simulávi, vos ut pértemptarem. **DA.** Quíd aïs? **SI.** Sic
res ést. **DA.** (*With affected admiration.*) Vide:
Numquam ístuc quivi ego íntellegere. váh, consilium
cállidum! 10
SI. Hoc aúdi: ut hinc te intro íre iussi, oppórtune hic
fit mi óbviam. **DA.** (*Aside, in consternation.*)
Hem, 590
Num nám perimus? **SI.** Nárro huic, quae tu dúdum
narrastí mihi.
DA. (*Aside.*) Quid nam aúdio? **SI.** Gnatam út det oro,
víxque id exoro. **DA.** (*Aside.*) Óccidi.
SI. (*Suspiciously, having partly overheard Davos.*) Hem,

quíd dixti? **DA.** Optume ínquam factum. **SI.**
Núnc per hunc nullást mora.
CH. Domúm modo ibo, ut ádparetur dícam, atque huc
renúntio. (*Exit Chremes.*) 15
SI. Nunc te óro, Dave, quóniam solus mi éffecisti has
núptias, 595
DA. (*Aside, in a tone of despair.*) Ego véro solus. **SI.**
gnátum mihi corrígere porro enítere.
DA. Faciam hércle seduló. **SI.** Potes nunc, dum ánimus
inritátus est.
DA. Quiéscas. **SI.** Age igitúr, ubi nunc est ípsus?
DA. Mirum ní domist.
SI. Ibo ád eum atque eadem haec, quaé tibi dixi, dícam
itidem illi. (*Exit Simo into his house.*) **DA.**
Núllŭs sum. 20
Quid caúsaest, quin hinc ín pistrinum récta proficiscár via?
Nil ést preci locí relictum: iám perturbavi ómnia: 601
Erúm fefelli: in núptias coniéci erilem fílium;
Feci hódie ut fierent, ínsperante hoc átque invito Pámphilo.
Em ăstútias! quod sí quiessem, níl evenissét mali. 25
(*The door of Simo's house opens.*) Sed éccum video ipsum:
óccidi. 605
Vtinám mihi esset áliquid hic, quo núnc me praecipitém darem.

SC. 5.

PAMPHILVS. DAVOS.

(*Pamphilus bursts out of the house, not seeing Davos.*)
PA. Vbi íllic est? scelús, qui me . . . (*Making a gesture of
despair.*) **DA.** (*Aside.*) Perii. **PA.** Átque hoc
confiteór iure

Mi óbtigisse, quándoquidem tam inérs, tam nulli cónsili
    sum :
Sérvon fortunás meas me cómmisisse fúttili!
Ego prétium ob stultitiám fero: sed inúltum numquam id
    aúferet.   610
DA. (*Aside*.) Postháč incolumem sát scio fore mé, si
    devito hóc malum.   5
PA. Nam quíd ego nunc dicám patri? negábon velle
    mé, modo
Qui súm pollicitus dúcere? qua fidúcia id facere aúdeam?
Nec quíd me nunc faciám scio. DA. (*Aside*.) Nec mé
    quidem, ătque id ago sédulo.
Dicam áliquid me inventúrum, ut huic malo áliquam pro-
    ducám moram.   615
PA. (*Catching sight of Davos*.) Oh. DA. (*Aside*.) Vísus
    sum. PA. Eho dúm bone vir, quid aís? viděn
    me tuis cónsiliis   10
Miserum ínpeditum esse? DA. Át iam expediam. PA.
    Expédies? DA. Certe, Pámphile.
PA. Nempe út modo. DA. Immo mélius spero. PA.
    Oh, tíbi ego ut credam, fúrcifer?
Tu rem ínpeditam et pérditam restítuas? em quo frétŭs
    sim,
Qui me hódie ex tranquillíssuma re cóniecisti in núptias. 620
Án non dixi esse hóc futurum? DA. Díxti. PA. Quid
    meritú's? DA. Crucem.   15
Séd sine paululum ád me redeam: iam áliquid dispiciam.
    PA. Eí mihi,
Quóm non habeo spátium, ut de te súmam supplicium,
    út volo:
Námque hoc tempus praécavere míhi me, haud te ulciscí
    sinit.

ACTVS IV.

SC. 1.

CHARINVS. PAMPHILVS. DAVOS.

(*Charinus enters in great agitation. Pamphilus and Davos are at the back of the stage.*)

CH. Hócinĕst crédibile aút memorábile, 625
Tánta vecórdia innáta quoiquam út siet,
Vt malis gaúdeant átque ĕx incómmodis
Álteriús sua ut cómparent cómmoda? ah
Ídnĕst verum? ímmo id hominúmst genus péssumum, 5
Dénegandí modō quís pudor paúlum adest: 630
Póst ubī témpŭs promíssa iam pérfici,
Túm coactí necessário se áperiunt:
[Et timent, et tamen res premit denegare]
Íbi tum eorum ínpudentíssuma orátiost: 10
 'Quís tu es? quis mihi es? quór meam tibi? 635
 Heus, próxumus sum egomét mihi.'
At tamen 'ubí fides?' sí roges, nīl pudet
Hic úbi opus est: illíc ubī nil ópus est, ibi veréntur.
Séd quid agam? adeámne ad eum et cum eo iniúriam
 hanc expóstulem? 15
Íngeram mala múlta? atque aliquis dícat 'nil pro-
 móveris': 640
Multúm: molestus cérte ei fuero atque ánimo morem
 géssero.
PA. Charíne, et me et te inprúdens, nisi quid dí re-
 spiciunt, pérdidi.

CH. (*Bitterly*.) Ítane 'inprudens'? tándem inventast caúsa.
solvistí fidem.
PA. Quíd 'tandem'? CH. Etiam núnc me ducere ístis
dictis póstulas? 20
PA. Quíd ístuc est? CH. Postquám me amare díxi, com-
placitást tibi. 645
Ileú me miserum, quí tuom animum ex ánimo spectaví meo.
PA. Fálsus's. CH. Non tibí satis esse hoc vísum soli-
dumst gaúdium,
Nísi me lactassés amantem et fálsa spe prodúceres.
Hábeas. PA. Habeam? ah néscis quantis ín malis vorsér
miser, 25
Quantásque hic suis consíliis mihi confécit sollicitúdines 650
Meus cárnufex. (*Shaking his fist at Davos.*) CH. (*Sarcas-
tically.*) Quid ístúc tam mirumst, dé te si exem-
plúm capit?
PA. Haud ístuc dicas, sí cognoris vél me vel amorém meum.
CH. Scio: cúm patre altercásti dudum, et ís nunc prop-
tereá tibi
Suscénset nec te quívit hodie cógere illam ut dúceres. 30
PA. Immo étiam, quo tu mínŭs scis aerumnás meas, 655
Haec núptiae non ádparabantúr mihi:
Nec póstulabat núnc quisquam uxorém dare.
CH. Scio: tú coactus tuá voluntate és. (*Turns upon his
heel and is going off.*) PA. Mane:
Nondúm scis. CH. Scio equidem íllam ducturum ésse te. 35
PA. Quor me énicas? hoc aúdi. numquam déstitit 660
Instáre, ut dicerém me ducturúm patri:
Suadére, orare usque ádeo donec pérpulit.
CH. Quis homo ístuc? PA. Davos. CH. Dávos? PA.
Intertúrbat. CH. Quam ob rem? PA. Néscio,
Nisi mí deos satís sció fuisse irátos, qui auscultáverim. 40

CH. Factum hóc est, Dave? **DA.** Fáctum. **CH.** Hem,
    quid aís, scelus?   665
At tíbi di dignum fáctis exitiúm duint.
Eho, díc mihi, si omnes húnc coniectum in núptias
Inimíci vellent, quód nisi consilium hóc darent?
DA. Decéptus sum, at non défetigatús. **CH.** Scio.   45
DA. Hac nón successit, ália adgrediemúr via: 670
Nisi íd putas, quia prímo processít parum,
Non pósse iam ad salútem convorti hóc malum.
PA. Immo étiam: nam satís crédo, si advigiláveris,
Ex únis geminas míhi conficies núptias.   50
DA. Ego, Pámphile, hoc tibi pró servitio débeo,   675
Conári manibus pédibus noctisque ét dies,
Capitís periclum adíre, dum prosím tibi:
Tuomst, síquid praeter spem évenit, mi ignóscere.
Parúm succedit quód ago: at facio sédulo.   55
Vel mélius tute réperi, me missúm face.   680
PA. Cupió: restitue quem á me accepistí locum.
DA. Faciam. **PA.** Át iam hoc opus est. **DA.** Séd manĕ:
    concrepúit a Glycerio óstium.
PA. Nil ád te. **DA.** (*Assuming an attitude of deep thought.*)
    Quaero. **PA.** Hem, núncine demum? **DA.** At
    iam hóc tibi inventúm dabo.

SC. 2.

MYSIS. PAMPHILVS. CHARINVS. DAVOS.

(*Mysis, coming out of Glycerium's house, speaks through the
door to Glycerium within.*)
  MY. Iam ubi úbi erit, inventúm tibī curábo et mecum
    addúctum

Tuom Pámphilum : tu módo, anime mi, nolí te macerare. 685
PA. Mysís. **MY.** Quis est? hem Pámphile, optumé mihi
te offers. **PA.** Quíd *id* est?
MY. Oráre iussit, sí se ames, erá, iam ut ad sese vénias:
Vidére aït te cúpere. **PA.** (*Aside.*) Vah, perii : hóc malum
integráscit. 5
(*To Davos.*) Sicíne me atque illam operá tua nunc míseros
sollicitári!
Nam idcírco arcessor, núptias quod mi ádparari sénsit. 690
CH. (*Bitterly.*) Quibŭs quídĕm quam facile pótuerat quiésci,
si hic quiésset!
DA. Age, si híc non insanít satis sua spónte, instiga.
MY. Atque édepol
Ea rés est: propterеáque nunc misera ín maerorest. **PA.**
(*With great emotion.*) Mýsis, 10
Per ŏmnís tibi adiuró deos, numquam eám me desertúrum,
Non, sí capiundos míhi sciam esse inimícos omnis hómines.
Hanc mi éxpetivi, cóntigit : convéniunt mores: váleant 696
Qui intér nos discidiúm volunt : hanc nísi mors mi adimet
némo.
MY. Resipísco. **PA.** Non Apóllinis magïs vérum atque
hoc respónsumst. 15
Si póterit fieri, ut né pater per mé stetisse crédat,
Quo mínus haec fierent núptiae, voló. sed si id non
póterit, 700
Id fáciam, in procliví quod est, per mé stetisse ut crédat.
Quis vídeor? **CH.** Miser, aeque átque egō. **DA.** Con-
sílium quaero. **CH.** Fórti's.
PA. (*Sneeringly.*) Scio, quíd conere. **DA.** Hoc égo tibī
profécto effectum réddam. 20
PA. Iam hoc ópus est. **DA.** Quin iam habeó. **CH.** Quid
est? **DA.** Huic, nón tibi habeo, ne érres.

CH. Sat hábeo. **PA.** Quid faciés? cedō. **DA.** Dies híc
    mi ut satís sit véreor   705
Ad agéndum : ne vacuom ésse me nunc ád narrandum
    crédas :
Proinde hínc vos amolímini : nam mi ínpedimento éstis.
PA. Ego hănc vísam. (*Exit into Glycerium's house.*) **DA.**
    Quid tu? quo hínc te agis? **CH.** Verúm vis
    dicam? **DA.** Immo étiam   25
Narrátionis íncipit mi inítium. **CH.** Quid me fíet?
DA. Eho tu ínpudens, non sátis habes, quod tíbi dieculam
    áddo,   710
Quantum huíc promoveo núptias? **CH.** Dave, át tamen
    DA. Quid érgo?
CH. Vt dúcam. **DA.** Ridiculum. **CH.** Húc face ad me
    ut vénias, siquid póteris.
DA. Quid véniam? nil habeo. **CH.** Át tamen siquíd. **DA.**
    Age, veniam. **CH.** Síquid,   30
Domi eró. (*Exit at back of stage.*) **DA.** Tu, Mysis, dum
    éxeo, parúmper me opperíre hic.
MY. Quaprópter? **DA.** Ita factóst opus. **MY.** Matúra.
    DA. Iam inquam hic ádero. (*Exit into Glycerium's
    house.*)   715

SC. 3.

MYSIS. DAVOS.

MY. Nilne ésse proprium quoíquam! di vostrám fidem :
Summúm bonum esse eraé putavi hunc Pámphilum,
Amícum, amatorém, virum in quovís loco

Parátum: verum ex eó nunc misera quém capit
Labórem! facile hic plús malist quam illíc boni.   5 720
(*Re-enter Davos with the baby in his arms.*) Sed Dávos exit.
    mi hómo, quid istuc óbsecrost?
Quo pórtas puerum? DA. (*Mysteriously.*) Mýsis, nunc
    opus ést tua
Mihi ad hánc rem exprompta málitia atque astútia.
MY. Quid nam íncepturu's? DA. Áccipe a me hunc
    ócius
Atque ánte nostram iánuam adpone. MY. Óbsecro, 10 725
Humíne? DA. Ex ara hinc súme verbenás tibi
Atque eás substerne. MY. Quam ób rem id tute nón
    facis?
DA. Quia, sí forte opŭs sit ád erum iurandúm mihi
Non ádposuisse, ut líquido possim. MY. Intéllego:
(*Sarcastically.*) Nova núnc religio in te ístaec incessít.
    cedo.   15 730
DA. Move ócius te, ut quíd agam porro intéllegas.
(*Looking round.*) Pro Iúppiter. MY. Quid ĕst? DA.
    Spónsae pater intérvenit.
Repúdio quod consílium primum inténderam.
MY. Nesció quid narres. DA. Égo quoque hinc ab déx-
    tera
Veníre me adsimulábo: tu ut subsérvias   20 735
Orátioni, ut quómque opŭs sit, verbís vide.
MY. Ego quíd agas nil intéllego: sed síquid est,
Quod méa opera opus sit vóbis, aut tu plús vides,
Manébo, nequod vóstrum remorer cómmodum. (*Exit Da-
    vos, on the right, unseen by Chremes, who enters on
    the left.*)

SC. 4.

CHREMES. MYSIS. DAVOS.

CH. Revórtor, postquam quae ópŭs fuere ad núptias 740
Gnataé paravi, ut iúbeam arcessi. (*Seeing the baby.*) séd
    quid hoc?
Puer hérclest. mulier, tu ádposuisti hunc? **MY.** (*Aside.*)
    V́bi ĭllic est?
CH. Non mĭhi respondes? **MY.** (*Aside.*) Núsquam est.
    vae miseraé mihi,
Relíquit mĕ homo atque ábiit. **DA.** (*Entering hurriedly.*)
    Di vostrám fidem, 5
Quid túrbaest apŭd forúm? quid ĭlli hominum lĭtigant? 745
Tum annóna carast. (*Aside.*) quĭd dicam aliud, néscio.
MY. Quor tu óbsecro hic me sólam? **DA.** (*Loudly,
    feigning surprise at sight of the baby.*) Hem,
    quae haec est fábula?
Eho Mýsis, puer hic úndest? quisve huc áttulit?
MY. Satĭn sánu's, qui me id rógites? **DA.** Quem ego
    igitúr rogem, 10
Qui hic néminem alium vídeam? **CH.** (*Aside, having with-
    drawn to the back of the stage.*) Miror, únde sit. 750
DA. (*Shouting.*) Dictúra es quod rogo? **MY.** Aú. **DA.**
    (*Whispering.*) Concede ad déxteram.
MY. Delíras: non tute ípse? **DA.** Verbum sí mihi
V́núm, praeter quam quód te rogŏ, faxís, cave.
(*Aloud.*) Male dícis? undest? (*Whispering.*) díc clare.
    MY. A nobís. **DA.** (*Laughing loudly.*) Hahae: 15
Mirúm vero, inpudénter mulier sí facit 755
Peregrína. **CH.** (*Aside.*) Ab Andriást haec, quantum intéllego.
DA. Adeón videmur vóbis esse idónei,

In quíbŭs sic inludátis? **CH.** (*Aside.*) Veni in témpore.
DA. Propera ádeo puerum tóllere hinc ab iánua: 20
(*Whispering.*) Mané: cavĕ quoquam ex ístoc excessís
   loco. 760
MY. Di te éradicent: íta me miseram térritas.
DA. Tibi égo dico an non? **MY.** Quíd vis? **DA.** At
   etiám rogas?
Cedo, quóium puerum hic ádposuisti? díc mihi.
MY. Tu néscis? **DA.** (*Whispering.*) Mitte id quód scio:
(*Aloud.*) dic quód rogo. 25
MY. Vostrí. **DA.** Quoius nostri? **MY.** Pámphili.
   CH. (*Aside.*) Hem. **DA.** Quid? (*Shouting.*)
   Pámphili? 765
MY. Eho, ăn nón est? **CH.** (*Aside.*) Recte ego sémper
   fugi has núptias.
DA. (*Bawling.*) O fácinus animadvórtendum. **MY.** Quid
   clámitas?
DA. Quemne égo heri vidi ad vós adferri vésperi?
MY. O hóminem audacem. **DA.** Vérum: vidi Cántharam 30
Suffárcinatam. **MY.** Dís pol habeo grátiam, 770
Quom in páriundo aliquot ádfuerunt líberae.
DA. Ne illa íllum haud novit, quóius causa haec íncipit:
'Chremés si positum púerum ante aedis víderit,
Suam gnátam non dabít': tanto hercle mágis dabit. 35
CH. (*Aside.*) Non hércle faciet. **DA.** Núnc adeo, ut tu
   sís sciens, 775
Nisi púerum tollis, iám ego hunc in mediám viam
Provólvam teque ibídem pervolvam ín luto.
MY. Tu pól homo non es sóbrius. **DA.** Fallácia
Alia áliam trudit. iám susurrari aúdio, 40
Civem Átticam esse hanc. **CH.** (*Aside.*) Hém. **DA.** 'Co-
   actus légibus 780

Eam uxórem ducet.' MY. Óbsecro, an non cívis est?
CH. (*Aside.*) Ioculárium in malum ínsciens paene íncidi.
DA. (*Turning round.*) Quis hĭc lóquitur? O Chremés, per
    tempus ádvenis:
Auscúlta. CH. Audivi iam ómnia. DA. (*With affected
    surprise.*) Anne haec tu ómnia?   45
CH. Audívi, inquam, a princípio. DA. Audistin, óbsecro?
    hem   785
Scelera, hánc iam oportet ín cruciatum hinc ábripi.
Hic ēst ílle: non te crédas Davom lúdere.
MY. Me míseram: nil pol fálsi dixi, mí senex.
CH. Novi ómnem rem. est Simo íntus? DA. Est. (*Exit
    Chremes into Simo's house. Davos lays his hand
    on Mysis' shoulder.*) MY. Ne me áttigas,   50
Sceléste. si pol Glýcerio non ómnia haec . .   790
DA. Eho inépta, nescis quíd sit actum? MY. Quí sciam?
DA. Hic sócer est. alio pácto haud poterat fíeri,
Vt scíret haec quae vóluimus. MY. Praedíceres.
DA. Paulum ínteresse cénses, ex animo ómnia,   55
Vt fért natura, fácias an de indústria?   795

SC. 5.

CRITO. MYSIS. DAVOS.

(*Crito comes on from Peiraeus: he gazes around.*)
CR. In hác habitasse plátea dictumst Chrýsidem.
Eius mórte ea ad me lége redierúnt bona.   799
(*Seeing Mysis and Davos.*) Sed quós perconter vídeo. sal-
    vete. MY. (*Excited and trembling.*) Óbsecro,   5

Quem vídeo? estne hic Critó sobrinus Chrýsidis?
Is ést. **CR.** O Mysis, sálve. **MY.** Salvos sís, Crito.
CR. Ităn Chrýsis? hem. **MY.** (*Weeping.*) Nos quídĕm pol
    miseras pérdidit.
CR. Quid vós? quo pacto hic? sátine recte? **MY.** Nós-
    ne? sic:
Vt químus, aiunt, quándo ut volumus nón licet.   10 805
CR. Quid Glýcerium? iam hic suós parentis répperit?
MY. Vtinam.   **CR.** Án nondum etiam? haud aúspicato
    huc me ádpuli:
Nam pól, si id scissem, númquam huc tetulissém pedem:
Sempér enim dictast ésse haec atque habitást soror:
Quae illíus fuerunt, póssidet: nunc me hóspitem   15 810
Litís sequi, quam id míhi sit facile atque útile,
Aliórum exempla cómmonent: simul árbitror,
Iam aliquem ésse amicum et défensorem ei: nám fere
Grandiúscula iam proféctast illinc. clámitent
Me sýcophantam, heréditatem pérsequi   20 815
Mendícum: tum ipsam déspoliare nón lubet.
MY. O óptume hospes, pól Crito antiquom óbtines.
CR. Duc me ád eam, quando huc véni, ut videam. **MY.**
    Máxume. (*Exeunt into Glycerium's house.*)
DA. Sequar hós: me nolo in témpore hoc videát senex.
                      (*Exit.*)

ACTVS V.

SC. 1.

CHREMES. SIMO.

(*Chremes comes out of Simo's house, followed by Simo himself.*)

CH. Sátĭs iam satĭs, Simó, spectata ergá te amicitiást
  mea :   820
Sátĭs pericli incépi adire : orándi iam finém face.
Dúm studeo obsequí tibi, paene inlúsi vitam fíliae.
SI. Ímmo enim nunc quom máxume abs te póstulo atque
  oró, Chremes,
V́t beneficium vérbis initum dúdum nunc re cómprobes. 5
CH. Vídĕ quam iniquos sís prae studio : dum íd efficias
  quód cupis,   825
Néque modum benígnitatis néque quid me ores cógitas :
Nám si cogités, remittas iám me onerare iniúriis.
SI. Quíbus? **CH.** (*Indignantly.*) At rogitas? pérpulisti me,
  út homini adulescéntulo
Ín alio occupáto amore, abhórrenti ab re uxória, 10
Fíliam ut darem ín seditionem átque in íncertas núptias, 830
Eíus labore atque eíus dolore gnáto ut medicarér tuo :
Ínpetrasti : incépi, dum res tétulit. nunc non fért : feras.
Íllam hinc civem esse áiunt : puer est nátus : nos missós
  face.
SI. Pér ego te deos óro, ut ne illis ánimum inducas cré-
  dere,   15
Quíbus id maxume útilest, illum ésse quam detérrumum.
Núptiarum grátia haec sunt fácta atque incepta ómnia. 836

Úbi ea causa, quam ób rem haec faciunt, érit adempta his, désinent.

CH. Érras: cum Davo égomet vidi iúrgantem ancillám.
SI. (*Scornfully.*) Scio.
CH. Véro voltu, quom íbi me adesse neúter tum praesén-
serat. 20
SI. Crédo, et id factúras Davos dúdum praedixít mihi:
Ét nescio qui tíbi sum oblitus hódie, ac volui, dícere. 841

SC. 2.

DAVOS. CHREMES. SIMO. DROMO.

(*Davos comes out of Glycerium's house, not seeing Chremes and Simo, who draw back. Davos speaks through the door to Glycerium within.*)

DA. Ánimo nunciam ótioso esse ínpero CH. (*Apart to Simo.*) Em Davóm tibi.
SI. (*Apart.*) Únde egreditur? DA. meó praesidio atque hóspitis. SI. (*Apart.*) Quid illúd malist?
DA. (*Turning to the audience.*) Égo commodiorem hómi-
nem, adventum, témpus, non vidí. SI. (*Apart.*) Scelus,
Quém nam hic laudat? DA. Ómnis res est iam ín vado.
SI. (*Apart.*) Cesso ádloqui? 845
DA. (*Catching sight of Simo.*) Érus est: quid agam? SI. (*Sneeringly.*) O sálve, bone vir. DA. (*Confused.*) Éhĕm Simo, O nostér Chremes, 5
Ómnia adparáta iam sunt íntus. SI. Curastí probe.
DA. Úbi voles, arcésse. SI. Bene sane: íd enim vero hinc núnc abest.

(*Changing his tone.*) Étiam tu hoc respónde, quid ístic
    tíbi negotist? **DA.** Míhin? **SI.** Ita.
DA. Míhin? **SI.** Tibi ergo. **DA.** Módo *ego* intro ivi.
    SI. Quási ego quam dudúm rogem.   850
DA. Cúm tuo gnato una. **SI.** (*In a tone of anger and
    distress.*) Ánne est intus Pámphilus? cruciór
    miser.   10
Ého, non tu dixti ésse inter eos ínimicitias, cárnufex?
DA. Súnt. **SI.** Quor igitur híc est? **CH.** (*Ironically.*)
    Quid íllum cénses? cum illa lítigat.
DA. (*With exaggerated solemnity.*) Ímmo vero indígnum,
    Chremës, iam fácinus faxo ex me aúdias.
Néscio qui senéx modo venit: éllum, confidéns, catus: 855
Quóm faciem videás, videtur ésse quantivís preti: 15
Tristís severitás inest in vóltu atque in verbís fides.
SI. Quíd nam adportas? **DA.** Níl equidem, nisi quód
    illum audivi dícere.
SI. Quíd aït tandem? **DA.** Glýcerium se scíre civem esse
    Átticam. **SI.** Hem,
(*Shouting into his house.*) Dromó, Dromo. **DA.** Quid ést?
    SI. Dromo. **DA.** Audi. **SI.** (*Storming about
    the stage.*) Vérbum si addideris.. Dromo.   860
DA. Audi óbsecro. (*Enter Dromo.*) **DR.** Quid vís? **SI.**
    Sublimem hunc íntro rape, quantúm potest.   20
DR. Quem? **SI.** Dávom. **DA.** Quam ob rem? **SI.** Quía
    lubet. rape ínquam. **DA.** Quid fecí? **SI.** Rape.
(*Dromo seizes Davos, and after a short struggle lifts him
    from the ground.*)
DA. Si. quícquam invenies mé mentitum, occídito. **SI.**
    Nil aúdio:
Égo iam te commótum reddam. **DA.** Támen etsi hoc
    verúmst? **SI.** Tamen.

Cura ádservandum vínctum, atque audin? quádrupedem
        constríngito.   865
Age núnciam: (*Davos is carried off: Simo shouts after him.*)
        ego pol hódie, si vivó, tibi   25
Osténdam, erum quid sít pericli fállere,
(*Shaking his fist at Glycerium's house.*) Et ĭllí patrem.
CH. Ah ne saévi tanto opere. **SI.** (*Leaning on
Chremes' shoulder, quite overcome.*) Ó Chremes,
Pietátem gnati! nónne te miserét mei?
Tantúm laborem cápere ob talem fílium?   870
(*Calling into Glycerium's house.*) Age Pámphile, exi Pám-
        phile: ecquid té pudet?   30

SC. 3.

PAMPHILVS. SIMO. CHREMES.

(*Pamphilus comes out hastily.*)

PA. Quis mé volt? perii, páter est. **SI.** Quid aïs, óm-
        nium..? **CH.** Ah,
Rem pótius ipsam díc, ac mitte mále loqui.
SI. Quasi qufcquam in hunc iam grávius dici póssiet.
Aïn tándem, civis Glýceriumst? **PA.** Ita praédicant. 875
SI. (*Sneeringly.*) 'Ita praédicant'? (*Bursting out passion-
        ately.*) O ingéntem confidéntiam!   5
Num cógitat quid dícat? num factí piget?
Vidĕ num efus color pudóris signum usquam índicat.
Adeo fnpotenti esse ánimo, ut praeter cívium
Morem átque legem et suí voluntatém patris   880
Tamen hánc habere stúdeat cum summó probro! 10

PA. Me míserum! **SI.** (*Mournfully.*) Hem, modone id
démum sensti, Pámphile?
Olim ístuc, olim, quom íta animum induxtí tuom,
Quod cúperes aliquo pácto efficiundúm tibi:
Eodém die istuc vérbum vere in te áccidit. 885
(*Bitterly.*) Sed quíd ego? quor me excrúcio? quor me
mácero? 15
Quor meám senectutem huíus sollicito améntia?
An ŭt pro huíus peccatis égo supplicium súfferam?
Immo hábeat, valeat, vívat cum illa. **PA.** Mí pater.
SI. Quid 'mí pater'? quasi tu húius indigeás patris. 890
Domus, úxor, liberi ínventi invitó patre. 20
Addúcti qui illam cívem hinc dicant: víceris.
PA. Patér, licetne paúca?' **SI.** Quid dicés mihi?
CH. Tamén, Simo, audi. **SI.** Ego aúdiam? quid aúdiam,
Chremés? **CH.** At tandem dícat. **SI.** (*Yielding with a bad
grace.*) Age, dicát·sino. 895
PA. Égo me amare hanc fáteor: si id peccárest, fateor íd
quoque. 25
Tíbi, pater, me dédo. quidvis óneris inpone, ínpera.
Vís me uxorem dúcere? hanc vis míttere? ut poteró, feram.
Hóc modo te obsecro, út ne credas á me adlegatum húnc
senem:
Síne me expurgem atque íllum huc coram addúcam. **SI.**
Adducas? **PA.** Síne, pater. 900
CH. Aéquom postulát: da veniam. **PA.** Síne te hoc exo-
rém. **SI.** Sino. (*Exit Pamphilus into Glycerium's
house.*) 30
Quídvis cupio, dúm ne ab hoc me fálli comperiár, Chremes.
CH. Pró peccato mágno paulum súpplici satis ést patri.

SC. 4.

CRITO. CHREMES. SIMO. PAMPHILVS.

(*Crito, coming out of Glycerium's house, speaks to Pamphilus, who follows.*)

CR. Mítte orare. una hárum quaevis caúsa me ut faciám monet,
Vél tu vel quod vérumst vel quod ípsi cupio Glýcerio. 905
CH. (*Astonished.*) Ándrium ego Critónem video? cérte is ěst. CR. Salvos sís, Chreme.
CH. Quíd tu Athenas ínsolens? CR. Evénit. sed hicinést Simo?
CH. Híc. CR. Simo, men quaéris? SI. (*In a loud and rude tone.*) Eho tu, Glýcerium hinc civem ésse aïs? 5
CR. Tú negas? SI. Itane húc paratus ádvenis? CR. Qua ré? SI. (*Working himself into a passion.*) Rogas?
Túne inpune haec fácias? tune hic hómines adulescéntulos 910
Ínperitos rérum, eductos líbere, in fraudem ínlicis?
Sóllicitando et póllicitando eorum ánimos lactas? CR. Sánun es?
SI. Ác meretriciós amores núptiis conglútinas? 10
PA. (*Aside.*) Périi, metuo ut súbstet hospes. CH. Sí, Simo, hunc norís satis,
Nón ita arbitráre: bonus est híc vir. SI. (*Sneeringly.*) Hic vir sít bonus? 915
Ítane attemperáte evenit, hódie in ipsis núptiis
Vt veniret, ántehac numquam? est véro huic credundúm, Chremes.
PA. (*Aside.*) Ní metuam patrem, hábeo pro illa re íllum quod moneám probe. 15

E

SI. Sýcophanta. **CR.** Hem. **CH.** Síc, Crito, est hic : mítte.
    CR. (*Indignantly.*) Videat quí siet.
Sí mihi perget quaé volt dicere, éa quae non volt aúdiet. 920
Égo ístaec moveo aut cúro? non tu tuóm malum aequo
    animó feres?
Nam égo quae dico véra an falsa audíerim, iam scirí potest.
Átticus quidam ólim nave frácta ad Andrum eiéctus est   20
Ét ístaec una párva virgo. túm ille egens forte ádplicat
Prímum ad Chrysidís patrem se. **SI.** (*Insultingly.*) Fábulam
    inceptát. **CH.** Sine.   925
CR. Ítane vero obtúrbat? **CH.** Perge. **CR.** Tum ís mihi
    cognatús fuit,
Qui cúm recepit. íbi ego audivi ex íllo sese esse Átticum.
Ís ibi mortuóst. **CH.** (*Eagerly.*) Eius nomen? **CR.** Nómen
    tam citó tibi? **PA.** (*Aside.*) Hem,   25
Perií. **CR.** Verum hercle opínor fuisse Phániam : hoc
    certó scio,
Rhamnúsium se aiébat esse. **CH.** (*Aside, but much excited.*)
    O Iúppiter. **CR.** Eadem haéc, Chreme,   930
Multi álii in Andro audívere. **CH.** (*Aside.*) Vtinam id sít,
    quod spero. (*Aloud.*) eho, díc mihi,
Quid eám tum? suamne esse aíbat? **CR.** Non. **CH.**
    Quoiam ígitur? **CR.** Fratris fíliam.
CH. Certé meast. **CR.** Quid aís? **SI.** Quid tǔ aïs? **PA.**
    (*Aside.*) Árrige auris, Pámphile.   30
SI. Qui crédis? **CH.** Phania íllic frater méus fuit. **SI.**
    Noram ét scio.
CH. Is béllum hinc fugiens méque in Asiam pérsequens
    proficíscitur :   935
Tum illám relinquere híc est veritus. póst illa nunc primum aúdio
Quid illó sit factum. **PA.** (*Aside.*) Víx sum apud me : ita
    ánimus commotúst metu

Spe gaúdio, mirándo hoc tanto tám repentinó bono. 35
SI. Ne istám multimodis tuam ínveniri gaúdeo. PA. Credó, pater.
CH. At mi únus scrupulus étiam restat, quí me male habet.
PA. (*Aside*.) Dígnus es 940
Cum tuá religione, ódium .. nodum in scírpo quaeris. CR. Quíd ístuc est?
CH. Nomén non convenít. CR. Fuit hercle huic áliud parvae. CH. Quód, Crito?
Numquíd meministi? CR. Id quaéro. PA. (*Aside*.) Egon huius mémoriam patiár meae 40
Volŭptáti obstare, quom égomet possim in hác re medicarí mihi?
Non pátiar. (*Aloud*.) heus, Chremés, quod quaeris, Pásiphi'last. CH. Ipsást. CR. East. 945
PA. Ex ípsa miliéns audivi. SI. Omnís nos gaudere hóc, Chremes,
Te crédo credere. CH. Íta me dí ament, crédo. PA. Quid restát, pater?
SI. Iam dúdum res reddúxit me ipsa in grátiam. PA. (*Clasping Simo's hand*.) O lepidúm patrem! 45
De uxóre, ita ut possédi, nil mutát Chremes? CH. Causa óptumast:
Nisi quíd pater aït áliud. PA. (*With a significant gesture*.) Nempe id? SI. Scílicet. CH. Dos, Pámphile, est 950
Decém talenta. PA. (*With effusion*.) Accípio. CH. Propero ad fíliam. eho mecúm, Crito:
Nam illám me credo haud nósse. (*Exeunt Chremes and Crito*.) SI. Quor non íllam huc transferrí iubes?
PA. Recte ádmones: Davo égo ístuc dedam iám negoti.
SI. Nón potest. 50

PA. Qui? SI. Quía habet aliud mágis ex sese et máius.
PA. Quid nam? SI. Vínctus est.
PA. Patér, non recte vínctust. SI. Haud ita iússi. PA.
Iubĕ solvi óbsecro. 955
SI. Age fíat. PA. At matúra. SI. Eo intro. (*Exit into his house.*) PA. O faústum et felicém diem!

'SC. 5.

CHARINVS. PAMPHILVS.

(*Charinus enters, unseen by Pamphilus.*)
CH. (*Aside.*) Províso quid agat Pámphilus: atque eccúm.
PA. (*Soliloquising.*) Aliquis me fórsitan
Putĕt nón putare hoc vérum: at mihi nunc síc esse hoc verúm lubet.
Égo deorum vítam eapropter sémpiternam esse árbitror,
Quód volŭptates córum propriae súnt: nam mi inmortálitas 960
Pártast, si nulla aégritudo huic gaúdio intercésserit. 5
Séd quem ego mihi potíssumum optem, quoí nunc haec narrém, dari?
CH. (*Aside.*) Quíd illud gaudist? (*The door of Simo's house opens.*) PA. Dávom video. némost, quem malim ómnium:
Nam húnc scio mea sólide solum gávisurum gaúdia.

SC. 6.

DAVOS. PAMPHILVS. CHARINVS.

(*Enter Davos, dejected, and much the worse for his punishment.*)
DA. Pámphilus ubi nam híc est? **PA.** Dave. **DA.** Quís
  homost? **PA.** Ego sum. **DA.** (*Groaning.*) O
  Pámphile.   965
PA. Néscis quid mi obtígerit. **DA.** Certe: séd quid mi
  obtigerít scio. (*Making painful contortions.*)
PA. Ét quidem ego. **DA.** More hóminum evenit, út quod
  sum nanctús mali
Priŭs rescisceres tu, quam ego illud quód tibi evenít boni.
PA. Méa Glycerium suós parentis répperit. **DA.** Factúm
  bene. **CH.** (*Aside.*) Hem.   5
PA. Páter amicus súmmus nobis. **DA.** Quís? **PA.** Chre-
  mes. **DA.** Narrás probe.   970
PA. Néc mora ullast, quín iam uxorem dúcam. **CH.**
  (*Aside.*) Num ille sómniat
Éa quae vigilans vóluit? **PA.** Tum de púero, Dave . .
  DA. (*Impatiently interrupting.*) Ah désine:
Sólus est quem díligant di. **CH.** (*Aside.*) Sálvos sum, si
  haec véra sunt.
Cónloquar. (*Comes forward.*) **PA.** Quis homo . . Ó Cha-
  rine, in témpore ipso mi ádvenis.   10
CH. Béne factum. **PA.** Audisti? **CH.** Ómnia. age, me
  in tuís secundis réspice.   975
Túos est nunc Chremés: facturum ˏquaé‿voles' scio ésse
  ómnia.
PA. Mémini: atque adeo lóngumst illum me éxpectare
  dum éxeat.

Séquere hac me intus: apúd Glycerium nunc ést. tu, Dave, abí domum,
Própera, arcesse hinc qui aúferant eam. quíd stas? quid cessás? DA. Eo. 15
(*Exeunt Pamphilus and Charinus into Glycerium's house. Davos addresses the audience.*)
Ne éxpectetis dum éxeant huc: íntus despondébitur: 980
Íntus transigétur, siquid ést quod restet. CANTOR. Plaúdite.

ALTER EXITVS ANDRIAE.

PA. Mémini: (*Chremes is seen coming out of Glycerium's house.*) atque adeo *ut vólui commodum húc senex exít foras.* (977)
Sécede illuc áliquantisper. CH. Dáve, sequere me hác. DA. Sequor. (*Charinus and Davos retire to back of stage.*)

PAMPHILVS. CHARINVS. CHREMES. DAVOS.

PA. Te éxpectabam: est dé tua re, quód agere ego tecúm volo.
Óperam dedí, ne me ésse oblitum dícas tuae gnatae álterae:
Tíbi me opinor ínvenisse dígnum te atque illá virum.
CHA. (*Apart.*) Périi, Dave: dé meo amore ac víta iam sors tóllitur. 985
CHR. Nón nova istaec míhi condiciost, sí voluissem, Pámphile. 5
CHA. (*Apart.*) Óccidi, Dave. DA. (*Apart.*) *Ah* manē.

ANDRIA.

CHA. (*Apart.*) Perii. **CHR.** Id quam ób rem non volui, éloquar.
Nón idcirco, quód eum omnino adfínem mihi nollem:
CHA. (*Apart.*) Hém. **DA.** (*Apart.*) Tace.
CHR. séd amicitia nóstra, quae est a pátribus nobis trádita,
Eíus non aliquam pártem studui abdúctam tradi líberis. 990
Núnc quom copia ác fortuna utríque ut obsequerér dedit, 10
Détur. **PA.** Bene factum. **DA.** (*Turning to Charinus.*)
Ádi ătque age homini grátias. **CHA.** Salvé, Chremes,
Meórum amicorum ómnium mi aequíssume:
Quid *dícam? nam illud* míhi non minus est gaúdio,
Quam *mi évenire núnc* id quod *ego* abs te éxpeto: 995
Me répperisse, ut hábitus antehac fuí tibi, 15
Eundém tuom animum. **PA.** Quom ád eum te adplicáveris,
Studium éxinde ut erit, túte existumáveris.
CHR. Aliénus abs te, tămĕn qui tu esses nóveram.
PA. Id ita ésse facere cóniecturam ex mé licet. 1000
CHR. Ita rés est. gnatam tíbi meam Philúmenam 20
Vxórem et dotis séx talenta spóndeo.
Agátur intus, síquid restet. ω *Plaúdite.*

METRA HVIVS FABVLAE HAEC SVNT

Ver. 1 ad 174 iambici senarii
,, 175 et 177 iambici octonarii
,, 176 iambicus quaternarius
,, 178 et 179 trochaici septenarii
,, 180 et 181 iambici octonarii
,, 182 trochaicus septenarius
,, 183 ad 195 iambici octonarii
,, 196 ad 198 iambici senarii
,, 199 ad 214 iambici octonarii
,, 215 ad 226 iambici senarii
,, 227 iambicus octonarius
,, 228 ad 233 trochaici septenarii
,, 234 ad 239 iambici octonarii
,, 240 et 244 iambici quaternarii
,, 241 et 242 trochaici septenarii
,, 243 iambicus octonarius
,, 245 et 247 trochaici octonarii
,, 246 trochaicus dimeter catalecticus
,, 248 ad 251 trochaici septenarii
,, 252 iambicus quaternarius
,, 253 ad 255 iambici octonarii
,, 256 ad 260 trochaici septenarii
,, 261 ad 269 iambici octonarii
,, 270 ad 298 iambici senarii
,, 299 et 300 iambici septenarii
,, 301 et 305 et 307 trochaici octonarii
,, 302 et 306 et 308 trochaici septenarii
,, 303 et 304 309 ad 315 iambici octonarii
,, 318 iambicus senarius
,, 319 ad 383 trochaici septenarii
,, 384 ad 393 iambici senarii
,, 394 ad 403 iambici octonarii
,, 404 ad 480 iambici senarii

Ver. 481 ad 484 bacchiaci tetrametri acatalecti
,, 485 iambicus dimeter catalecticus
,, 486 iambicus senarius
,, 487 ad 496 iambici octonarii
,, 497 et 498 iambici senarii
,, 499 ad 505 iambici octonarii
,, 506 iambicus septenarius
,, 507 ad 509 iambici octonarii
,, 510 ad 515 trochaici septenarii
,, 517 trochaicus dimeter catalecticus
,, 518 ad 523 trochaici septenarii
,, 524 ad 532 iambici senarii
,, 533 ad 536 iambici octonarii
,, 537 iambicus quaternarius
,, 538 ad 574 iambici senarii
,, 575 ad 581 iambici septenarii
,, 582 ad 604 et 606 iambici octonarii
,, 605 iambicus quaternarius
,, 607 et 608 trochaici octonarii
,, 609 trochaicus septenarius
,, 610 ad 620 iambici octonarii
,, 621 ad 624 trochaici septenarii
,, 625 dactylicus tetrameter acatalectus
,, 626 ad 634 cretici tetrametri acatalecti
,, 635 compositus ex duabus trochaicis tripodiis catalecticis
,, 636 iambicus quaternarius
,, 637 creticus tetrameter acatalectus
,, 638 iambicus septenarius
,, 639 et 640 trochaici septenarii
,, 641 et 642 iambici octonarii
,, 643 ad 649 trochaici septenarii
,, 650 ad 654 iambici octonarii
,, 655 ad 662 iambici senarii
,, 663 et 664 iambici octonarii
,, 665 ad 681 iambici senarii
,, 682 et 683 iambici octonarii
,, 684 ad 715 iambici septenarii
,, 716 ad 819 iambici senarii

Ver. 820 ad 856 trochaici septenarii
,, 857 iambicus octonarius
,, 858 et 859 trochaici septenarii
,, 860 ad 863 iambici octonarii
,, 864 trochaicus septenarius
,, 865 iambicus octonarius
,, 866 ad 895 iambici senarii
,, 896 ad 928 trochaici septenarii
,, 929 ad 958 iambici octonarii
,, 959 ad 992 trochaici septenarii
,, 993 ad 1003 iambici senarii.

NOTES

THE notices, called διδασκαλίαι, concerning the origin and first performance of the plays of Plautus and Terence, were inserted after the titles of the MSS. probably, by grammarians of the Augustan age.

Graeca, a *Comoedia palliata*, where the characters and scenes are Greek; opposed to *togata*.

Menandru = Μενάνδρου.

Ludis Megalensibus. These were the games celebrated April 4th–9th in honour of the μεγάλη μήτηρ, Cybele, whose worship was introduced into Rome 205 B.C.: Livy 29. 10, 11. Theatrical representations did not form part of this festival till 194 B.C.

Aed. Cur. These officials are mentioned, because it was their business to settle with the poet and contract with the managers of the company.

egere, 'brought out.'

Praen. = *Praenestinus*.

modos fecit, 'music by.'

Claudi, sc. *servos*. This man wrote the music for all the plays of Terence.

tibiis paribus tota, i.e. with one musical accompaniment throughout, unlike the Hauton Timorumenos, which was '*primum tibiis inparibus, deinde duabus dextris.*'

Prologue.

The six plays of Terence are headed by Prologues, in which the poet anticipates criticisms or defends himself against them; in two of them, the prologues to the Phormio and the Eunuchus, he also retorts by criticising the performances of his critic. It is clear that the Andria was already known to the public, or at least to some portion of it, because Terence states (see ll. 13–16) the ground on which it had been attacked; but we do not know how this knowledge had been got. The play may have been performed before 166 B.C.; and the prologue, which we have, may have been written for its second appearance, as was the case with the Hecyra. Yet it seems strange that Terence should make no mention of a previous performance, if one had really taken place, especially as he distinctly states that the Hecyra had been condemned on the stage, when it was first brought out (see prologue to that play). Therefore it seems more probable that the Andria, like the Eunuchus, was known merely from the private rehearsal before the Curule Aediles. This view receives strong confirmation, if we can accept the story told by Suetonius of the recitation before the poet Caecilius; for which see Introduction.

The prologues to the plays of Terence differ from those to the plays of Plautus in several points: (1) Terence's prologues are genuine, while nearly, if not quite, all of Plautus' prologues are spurious; (2) of the prologues of Plautus (twelve in number, if we count the two remaining lines belonging to the Pseudulus), nine contain an analysis of the plot, which Terence thought unnecessary; (3) Terence never mentions himself by name; we find the name of Plautus in the prologues to the Trinummus, Asinaria, Pseudulus.

---

1. **Poeta**, used by Terence in all his prologues instead of his own name.

quom. Always in Plautus and Terence. The Latin writers till the end of the republican period regularly avoided a *u* after *u* or *v*. So we have *parvolo* in 35, *relicuom* in 25 (see note). The correct form in Cicero is *cum*.

animum adpulit, cf. 446. *adpellere* commonly means 'to bring to land,' and Cicero gives the metaphor fully, de Orat. II. 154 *tamquam ad aliquem libidinis scopulum, sic tuam mentem ad philosophiam adpulisti*. The expression = '*se conferre*,' 'to devote oneself to.'

2. **id negoti**, 'this simple task;' cf. 521. The expression is of more limited meaning than *id negotium*, since the genitive is partitive. Terence often has similar phrases in a comic sense, just as diminutives are used; e.g. Haut. 848 *quid hominis es?* **negoti**. This form of the genitive of substantives in *-ius*, *-ium* is universal in all writers, till the elegiac poets Ovid and Propertius introduced *-ii*; finding, of course, such forms as *imperi* etc. unmanageable. So 44 *benefeci*. Adjectives in *-ius*, however, do not contract the genitive.

3. **fabulas**, instead of *fabulae*, by attraction. Cf. 26, 47. This attraction of a substantive into the case of the relative is common in Plautus also, and found in Vergil, Horace, Ovid.

fecisset bears the same relation to *credidit* that the fut. perf. would to a primary tense.

4. **multo**, with *aliter*.

intellegit. Note the *e* in this and one other compound of *lego*, *neglego*.

5. **prōlogis**, in spite of πρόλογος, would seem natural to a Latin ear, accustomed to such compounds as *proloqui*. So too *prōpinare* and Gr. προπίνειν.

scribundis. This older form of the gerund and gerundive is familiar in *iure dicundo, res repetundae, potiundi,* &c. The MS. authority is unanimous for *scribundis* here and for *scribendum* in 1.

operam abutitur, 'uses up his time.' *Abuti* in the older Latin, like the Gr. ἀποχρῆσθαι, meant not 'to misuse,' but 'to use entirely;' even Cicero, when he wishes to give the word the meaning 'misuse,' generally adds some adverb or equivalent expression. It is regularly followed by the accusative in the comic poets, by the ablative later. *Utor* and *potior* are sometimes followed by the accusative in the comic poets; *fungor* always by accusative, with one doubtful exception (Adel. 603); *fruor* always by ablative, except Haut. 401, where the accusative is found.

6. **qui,** an old form of the ablative, used by Plautus and Terence in several senses:—

(1) as a relative, referring to any gender and either number—'wherewith.' Cf. 512.

(2) as a final particle with a subjunctive expressing purpose—'in order that.' Cf. 307, 334, and the present passage.

(3) as an interrogative adverb—'how?' Cf. 150, 302.

(4) introducing curses (πῶς, *utinam*). Cf. Phor. 123; Plaut. Trin. 923, 997 (not common).

(5) as an indefinite particle with words of emphasis (πώς), 'somehow,' e.g. *hercle qui, edepol qui, quippe qui, et qui.* Cf. 148. It is commonly used by the later writers also in *atqui, alioqui,* &c.

argumentum narret, 'explain the plot,' the natural use of a prologue, though Terence's practice is to make this unnecessary by explaining the argumentum as far as is needful in the first scene of the play.

7. **veteris poetae.** This 'old poet' was Luscius Lanuvinus. Terence never mentions him by name, but refers to him as *poeta vetus* in the prologue to Phorm. 1 and 13, and, with the epithet *malevolus* added, in the prologue to Haut. 22.

8. **vitio dent,** 'impute as a fault.' 'The dative sometimes denotes the design and operation of a thing (that to which it *serves* and *tends*).' Madvig, § 249. So *vitio vertere, probo ducere,* &c. The subject of *dent* is the old poet and his party.

advortite is the reading of all the MSS.: *attendite* is given by Donatus.

9. **Menander.** See Introduction.

Perinthiam, a comedy named from one of the characters, a girl from Perinthus in Thrace, just as *Andria* means a girl from Andros.

10. To know one is to know both on account of their general similarity of plot.

11. **non ita**, 'not very,' a common phrase. The text perhaps gives the best arrangement of a somewhat doubtful line.

12. **oratione ac stilo**, 'execution and form.' *argumentum* means the material of the plot, *oratio* the manner in which it is worked out, *stilus* the form of the language. This last = the word '*scriptura*,' Phor. prologue 5.

13. **quae convenere**, 'all that he found suitable.'

in Andriam, of course with *transtulisse*.

14. **fatetur.** Bentley has a characteristic note: '*Quis fatetur? an Menander? Is enim nominativus in proximo est. Adde igitur in fine versus, ex Perinthia hic.* It is true that Terence constantly refers to himself in the prologue as *hic*, e. g. 19; but the subject of *fatetur* is quite clear without it. Bentley for the same reason alters *antehac* into *ante hic*, Phor. prol. 4.

transtulisse. The omission of *se* and other pronouns before the infin. is frequent in Terence, e. g. 145, 358, 394, 401, 470, etc.

15. **isti**, i. e. the critics.

disputant, 'maintain,' a rare use of the word followed by acc. and infin.

in eo, 'therein,' 'in doing so;' the words are best explained by referring them to *vituperant*, as in 94 *in ea re* refers to *conflictatur* of the preceding line. Latin writers generally use *in ea re, eius rei*, &c., instead of the ambiguous *in eo*, etc.

16. **contaminari**, lit. 'to bring into contact' (for *contagminare*, same stem as *tango*). This verb (but not the substantive *contaminatio*) is used here and in Haut. prol. 17 in the sense of amalgamating two plays into one. Later it always means, to stain,' 'to mar,' and thus is found Eun. 552. The charge of 'contaminating' is mentioned by Terence and admitted to be true in this prologue and in those to the Eunuchus and Adelphi; the latter is peculiar, because the originals, from which it is taken, are by different poets, viz. Menander and Diphilus. The charge is also admitted in the prologue to Hauton Timorumenos; though Terence tells us that that play, however, is *ex integra Graeca integram comoediam*.

17. 'Is not the result of all their wisdom, that they are wise in nothing?' An instance of oxymoron, such as is common in Greek; e. g. Menander's φρονῶν οὐδὲν φρονεῖ.

ne, as often in the older Latin, for *nonne*, which is little used by Plautus and Terence. Cf. 238 note.

18. **Naevium, Plautum, Ennium.** See Introduction. Note that they are put in chronological order. The poet probably means that he

has followed them as models (*auctores*), not in 'contaminating,' but merely in the free use of Greek material.

20, 21. 'And his true wish is to rival their freedom rather than the pedantic accuracy of his critics.'

22. dehinc, of future time (cf. 190), while *abhinc* is of past. The word is always monosyllabic in Plautus and Terence; later poets seem to have used it as they liked.

porro, 'in future.'

23. dicere. Possibly here and in 535 *nubere* we ought to scan the last syllable long, the old termination being -*rei*; but it seems that all undoubted instances of this lengthening (of which 437 *dicerē* is to be noted) occur when the word is followed by a strong pause. In 535 there is no pause at all after *nubere*, and no strong pause here. More probably we should scan *maledi | cerĕ ma | lefacta;* and so 267 *Pam | phile quid | .*

noscant, 'have to listen to.'

24. favete, sc. *linguis* = εὐφημεῖτε.

rem cognoscite, i.e. do not condemn without hearing, as you treated the Hecyra. See note on Prologue.

25. spei, monosyllable.

relicuom. This word is always of four syllables in the older writers; *rēlicuos* in Lucr. 1. 560 (cf. Munro's note). Catullus, Tibullus, Vergil, and Horace, unwilling either to lengthen the first syllable or unite the two last, avoid the word altogether. Later it is used as a trisyllable, e.g. by Juvenal.

26. de integro, 'anew'; so *ab integro, ex integro;* no notion of *integrae* as opposed to *contaminatae comoediae*. For case of *comoedias* cf. 3 note.

27. exigendae, 'hissed off.' So *exactus,* Hec. prol. 15.

prius, explained as = *potius;* cf. 'rather,' the comparative of 'rath' (= 'early'). It may = *prius quam spectatae sint.*

Act I. Scene 1.

Simo tells his freedman Sosia of the early life and disposition of his son Pamphilus; of the love of the latter for Glycerium, and its accidental discovery; of the consequent refusal of Chremes to allow his daughter Philumena to marry Pamphilus; finally, of his (Simo's) pretence that the match is nevertheless to take place, in order that he may test the obedience of his son.

Thus Terence, following his ordinary practice, uses the first scene to give us such information about the position of affairs as enables us to understand the action of the play.

28. **istaec,** i.e. the things which the slaves have brought in from the market.

29. **adesdum.** In later Latin this enclitic use of *dum* is confined to the negatives *nondum, nedum, vixdum,* to *dudum* and *interdum,* and the imperatives *agedum, agitedum.* It is used by the comic poets with all imperatives (e.g. *abidum* Haut. 249, *circumspicedum* Plaut. Trin. 146), with *cho* (184, 616). *Quidum* (interrogative) is found in Terence, e. g. Hec. 319, *primumdum* Plaut. Trin. 98. Whether *adesdum* etc. should be written in one word or two is an unimportant point, on which no agreement seems to have been made.

 volo, sc. *conloqui.* Cf. 45 (see note), 345, 536, 872.

 paucis (ablative), sc. *verbis,* a common ellipse, cf. 536 note; though *verbis* is sometimes expressed, e.g. Plaut. Mil. 374 *paucis verbis te volo,* Trin. 963 *te tribus verbis volo.*

 dictum puta, cf. Ovid, Met. 4. 477 *facta puta, quaecunque iubes.*

30. **nempe,** sc. *vis.*

 curentur, of cookery; used by Plautus also in this sense.

31. **ars,** sc. *coquendi.*

 hoc, ablative after *amplius.*

33. **eis,** sc. *artibus,* further explained by the substantives *fide et taciturnitate* in apposition. Wagner says, 'It is quite perverse to supply *artibus.*' But why perverse?

 artes = 'qualities.' Cf. Plaut. Trin. 72 *artes antiquae tuae.*

35. **a parvolo** = ἐκ παιδός. Cf. 539 *a parvis.*

36. **iusta ac clemens,** 'reasonable and mild.'

37. **ex,** 'instead of,' as often; e. g. Cic. Phil. 3. 9. 22 *ex oratore arator.*

38. **propterea quod,** 'because your service was given with the spirit of freedom.' Cf. Adel. 886 *servom haud inliberalem,* and Menander's line, ἐλευθέρως δούλευε, δοῦλος οὐκ ἔσει, 'For freedom's spirit makes the bondman free.'

 servibas. Terence and Plautus seem to have used *-ibam* or *-iebam* for the imperfect of the fourth conjugation almost at pleasure, e.g. 930 *aichat,* 932 *aibat,* and Phorm. 83 *serviebat;* but always *sciebam, nesciebam.* The shorter form is sometimes employed by later poets, e. g. *accibant,* by Lucretius; *audibant, custodibant,* by Catullus; *lenibat, nutribant, vestibat,* by Vergil; *audibat, mollibat,* by Ovid; *largibar,* by Propertius.

39. **pretium** = *praemium,* i. e. freedom.

40. **haud muto factum,** 'I wish no change in it,' i. e. 'I do not regret it.' Cf. 949 *de uxore nil mutat Chremes.* It is possible to join *factum* to *gaudeo;* (so Bentley, followed by Meissner). Then *muto* must stand absolutely, or at any rate without an object expressed, and

factum gaudeo may be illustrated by Plaut. Most. 5. 2. 26 (1147) *bene hercle factum, et factum gaudeo*. But *factum gaudeo si tibi quid feci aut facio* sounds rather feebly emphatic.

42 Scan et ĭd grátum fuīsse.

advorsum te = *tibi*.

habeo gratiam. Note the singular with *habeo* (unlike *ago*). The usage is so thoroughly accepted, that some editors change 770 and Plaut. Trin. 659 *summas habeo gratias* (read by every MS.), turning the latter into *summam habebo gratiam*. A limit, however, ought to be put upon this fearless support of rules by the banishment of all exceptions. The only other instance of the plural with *habeo*, Phor. 894 *gratias habeo atque ago*, is explained by the presence of *ago*. There is a play on *gratum* and *gratiam*, 'I am grateful that you are gratified by my service.'

43. Scan **sed hŏc mihi**.

hoc, 'these words,' i.e. the *commemoratio*.

44. **exprobratiost inmemori.** The verbal substantive is often followed by the same case as the verb. So Livy, 23. 35. 7 *exprobratio cuiquam*; Verg. Aen. 6. 542 *iter Elysium*. Still more remarkable is the use of the acc. by Plautus after *receptio, curatio, tactio* (very often after the latter).

45. **quin dic.** Note the following uses of *quin*:—

(1) 'why not?' either in direct or indirect questions;

(2) with imperatives as here: this use was a natural development of the first; for such a question as *quin taces?* is equivalent in sense to a command;

(3) in the common sense 'but that' after verbs expressing prevention, doubt, and the like with a negative;

(4) as a corroborative particle, 'indeed,' 'verily.' Cf. 704.

quid est, indic., not subjunct. Cf. 449, 849, 878. 'In conversational or animated languages a question is often put, logically, though not grammatically dependent on another verb or sentence, e.g. on such expletives as *dic mihi, cedo, responde, vide*, etc. So frequently in Plautus and Terence, even where later writers would make the question dependent and use the subjunctive.' Roby, School Latin Grammar, 751. In 705, *quid facies? cedo*, the mere order of the words removes all difficulty.

quid est quod = 'wherefore,' *quod* being acc. of respect.

me velis. The ellipse of some such word as *conloqui* seems the established explanation; but if the phrase stood in this passage only, we might be led by comparing l. 50 to supply *facere*, thus giving a very simple construction to *quod*.

47. **quas credis, etc.** = *hae nuptiae, quas credis esse, non sunt verae.* Cf. 3.

48. **quor**, the old spelling of *cur*, always in Plautus and Terence.

49. Simo divides his discourse into three heads, *gnati vitam*, 51–156; *consilium meum*, 157–167; *quid facere, etc.*, 168–170.

51. **nam** introduces the narrative, as γάρ in Greek. Bentley reads *ac*, Meissner *et* at the end of this line, thus making *fuit* a part of the protasis, and *studebat* (59) the apodosis. It seems simpler to leave the text as it is, so that *fuit* is apodosis. Simo begins afresh at 55. Nothing will make the passage run very smoothly; the repetition of *nam* seems to show a want of finish.

    excessit ex ephebis. Cf. Plaut. Merc. 61. The age of the ἔφηβοι at Athens was from 18 to 20. Cic. pro Arch. 3. 4 has *ex pueris excessit*, a translation of the Greek ἐκ παίδων ἐξῆλθεν, and de Or. 2. 326 he quotes this line, and admires the following passage (i. e. about the next fifty lines) as a *longa narratio*. He then speaks of the *brevitas* and *venustas* of *effertur, imus* (117).

52. **liberius** must scan *libriŭs*. Cf. *dextra* from *dextera*. This is surely more natural than to consider *vivendi* a dissyllable. The meaning of the comparative seems clear enough; but Bentley thought it nonsense and changed the word into *libera*.

    fuit, monosyllable.

    antea, not elsewhere in Terence or Plautus.

53. **qui scire**, etc., 'how could you have known (if you had wished) or learnt his character?'

    posses is a potential subjunctive. Cf. 135 note.

54. **magister**, the slave who took a boy to school and back, παιδαγωγός.

55. **plerique omnes**, 'almost all,' a strengthened form of *plerique*. Cf. Phor. 172, Plaut. Trin. 29.

56. **ut animum adiungant**, explanatory of *quod*. *Animum adiungere* is not found elsewhere; but Terence uses many verbs with *animum*, e. g. *adpellere* (1, 446), *adplicare* (193).

57. **alere**, instead of *alendi* after *studium*. Cf. Mad. §§ 417, 419. The construction is common in the comic poets, e. g. after *opera, lubido, occasio:* Terence has gerund and infin. together after the last, Phor. 885. Vergil has instances e. g. after *modus, cupido, tempus*. It is found in prose also; Cicero has *tempus abire, ratio amittere*, etc.

    canes ad venandum = *canes venaticos*.

    ad philosophos after *animum adiungant*. It is rather hard on the philosophers to make attendance at their teaching a mere alternative to the keeping of horses and hounds; but a Roman audience could not appreciate the joke as the Athenians would. There was no class at Rome answering to the Sophists.

58. **horum**, plural, because *quod* has been expanded in 56, 57.

nil. The accus. of neuter pronouns and adjectives is not uncommon after *studere*; cf. Haut. 382, Hec. 199. The construction is also used by Cicero and Livy. Cf. 157 note.

60. **non iniuria**, 'not without cause.' Cf. 378, Haut. 581.

61. **adprime**, almost confined to Plautus and Terence, and always used by them with adjectives.

nequid nimis = μηδὲν ἄγαν, a hackneyed Greek proverb. It is with commonplace reflections of this sort that Sosia, like a chorus, relieves the garrulity of Simo. Cf. 67, 68, and 142, 143.

62. **omnis**. Some strangely read *omnes* (nom.). It is far more simple to make the subject of all the infinitives the same. **perferre**, historic infin. Cf. 97, 147. 369. This construction is thoroughly characteristic of the style of Terence, who in this respect is, as Spengel remarks, the Sallust of early Latin. It will be noticed that he even uses the historic infin. co-ordinate with a finite verb. If the words *advorsus—illis* below were considered to be an interpolation, it would be possible to regard the infinitives as in apposition to *vita*.

63. **quibus—quomque**. Tmesis. Cf. 263, 455, 486.

sese dedere, 'comply with the wishes of.' Cf. 897.

64. **eōrum**, dissyllable. The arrangement of the first three words is rather uncertain; and some have suspected that *advorsus—illis* is an interpolation. Bentley has subjected the words to an unsparing criticism, and it must be admitted that the passage does not run very well. But it is quite in the character of Simo to enforce his point by the addition of a couple of participial clauses, in which he lingers on the merits of his son. At any rate they sound natural enough on the stage. Spengel, adding *esse* to *advorsus*, turns it into an infin. co-ordinate with *obsequi*, etc.; but there is no grammatical difficulty in the text.

65. **illis**. Bentley's correction *aliis* is unnecessary. The plural notion is already contained in *nemini*.

ita = *quod si facias*. The MSS. give *ita ut*, which seems very awkward. *ut* probably was introduced on the false analogy of such passages as 80 *ita ut fit*.

66. **invenias**. Cf. 571.

68. This line is quoted by Cicero, De Am. § 89, as a general sentiment without the qualifying words *hoc tempore*.

69. **muliĕr quaedam**, Chrysis, named in 105.

abhinc. Cf. 22 note.

70. **viciniae**, partitive gen. depending on *huc*, as often after *ubi, quo, nusquam*, etc. *huc viciniam* is a needless correction, and *huic viciniae*, given by the MSS., a good instance of a copyist's blunder.

71. **cognatorum neglegentia.** This means a good deal in the mouth of an Athenian. At Athens, if an orphan girl was left poor, the next of kin was bound by Solon's law to marry her or to provide a substantial dowry. Cf. Phor. 125. *Cognatus* is not used in the technical Roman sense, but as a translation of the Greek ἀγχιστεύς. The ἀγχιστεύς in this case was Crito, who appears 796. As a citizen of Andros he was not subject to the Athenian law; so there is no reason to suppose that it was his *legal* duty to provide for Chrysis at Andros. He does not appear to have objected to inheriting anything that she might have left at her death.

73. **ei**, interjection, = *hei*.

74. **duriter**, 'with hard work.' Adverbs in *-iter*, formed from adjectives in *-us*, are common in early Latin, e. g. *avariter, amiciter, munditer*; later the termination *-e* became usual, but note *humaniter* (as well as *humane*) and *naviter* as exceptions.

81. **esset**, from *esse*, not from *edere*, as suggested by the older commentators.

82. **egomet.** This omission of a verb of 'saying' is common in Terence. Cf. 336. So Verg. Aen. 1. 37 *haec secum*, 3. 99 *haec Phoebus*.

83. **habet.** The regular exclamation over a gladiator who had received a blow. So *hoc habet*, Plaut. Most. 715, Verg. Aen. 12. 296.

84. **venientis aut abeuntis**, i. e. on errands to and from the houses of their respective masters.

88. **quid**, as in common talk we sometimes begin an explanation with 'why.'

symbolam = συμβολή, called *collecta* by Cicero de Or. 2. 57. 233. It was the contribution of each individual to the common fund for the payment of a dinner. So Phor. 339 *asymbolus* = a person who dines without being obliged to pay.

90. **nil quicquam**, 'nothing whatever,' an emphatic pleonasm; cf. Phor. 80, 250, and elsewhere in Terence. It is impossible to suppose, with Mr. Papillon, that *quicquam* is an adverbial accusative in these passages. For though, as he points out, *nemo quisquam* is not certain from Eun. 226, the phrase is established by Eun. 1032, Hec. 67.

91. **enīmvéro**, 'of course,' 'naturally,' used also to express anger or impatience; cf. 206. This emphatic use of *enim*, sometimes at the beginning of a sentence, is common in Plautus and Terence; cf. Plaut. Trin. 1134 *enim me nominat*. The shortening of the second syllable

of *enimvero* seems regular in Terence. Phor. 528 is a very doubtful exception.

spectatum, 'tested,' cf. 820, Cic. Verres 2. 3. 78 *spectatio pecuniae;* but the metaphor can hardly be extended to *conflictatur.*

93. **ingeniis,** 'characters,' i. e. his friends; abstract for concrete. So Cic. Arch. 5 *de ingeniis iudicare* of persons.

eius, monosyllable.

94. **animus.** Note the change of subject.

in ea re. Cf. 15 note.

95. **scias, suae,** both monosyllables. So *scio* 653, 658. The second pers. subj. is used here in the general sense, as we say 'one may know,' not to address Sosia. Cf. Mad. § 370.

modum, 'control.'

97. **dicere,** histor. infin.; cf. 62 note.

fortunas, stronger than the sing.

98. **qui.** Note that *meas* = genitive of *ego;* the relative agrees with the meaning.

100. **ultro,** emphatic, because it was usual for the father of the intended bridegroom to make the first proposal, as Philto does, Plaut. Trin. 449. This is a good example of the meaning of *ultro.*

101. **dote summa,** cf. 951, where the amount is put at ten talents.

102. **despondi,** sc. *eum.* Commonly used of promising a *daughter* in marriage; but the ordinary arrangement has been inverted on account of the unparalleled enthusiasm of Chremes.

103. Some MSS. give *quid igitur obstat quor non verae fiant.* It is necessary on metrical grounds to omit *igitur* or *verae.* Bentley showed conclusively that *verae* ought to be omitted. It must have been brought into the text from 47 by some copyist, who did not understand that *fieri* = *verae esse;* in fact, that *fieri verae* is almost nonsense. Cf. 529, 543, where *fieri* stands alone with the same meaning.

104. **ferme in diebus paucis, quibus haec acta sunt,** 'almost within the few days in the course of which the contract was made.' Scarcely was the betrothal over, when the death of Chrysis and the consequent disclosure ruined the hope of Chremes.

106. **ibi tum,** pleonastic, as in 131, 223, 634. *ibi* is temporal, as also without *tum* 356, 379; frequent in Livy.

107. **qui amabant** = *amatores,* i. e. those who loved her when she was alive. *amarant* is an unnecessary correction.

frequens, used adverbially, = 'often.' *frequenter* is not found before Cicero.

110. **consuetudinis,** 'acquaintance.'

111. **tam fert familiariter,** 'feels with such tenderness.' Note the

unusual separation of *tam* from the adverb; but cf. Cic. Arch. 8. 17 *tam animo agresti.*

113. humani, 'sympathetic.'

115. eius, i. e. the son. Certainly not *humani ingeni*, etc.

prodeo. So *produco* is technically used of conducting a corpse to the grave.

116. etiam = 'yet,' with negative, as in 503. Cic. Tusc. 1. 12. Without negative = 'still.' Cf. 940. Verg. Aen. 6. 485 *Idaeumque etiam currus, etiam arma tenentem.*

117. effertur, often like ἐκφέρειν, used of funerals.

118. unam, prob. emphatic = 'one specially;' though *unus* sometimes seems to be used as equivalent to an indefinite article.

120. ut nil supra, sc. *esse posset.*

121. quia tum, needlessly altered into *quae tum* or *quae quom.* The repetition of *quia* like that of *praeter ceteras* (which happily has defied emendation) is in keeping with the general character of Simo's narrative.

123. honesta ac liberali, ' fair and ladylike.'

pedisequas, the waiting-women, who would naturally attend the funeral of their mistress. This seems to show that Chrysis was in better circumstances than we should have inferred from 74, 75. But the point need not be pressed.

125. percussit. Used almost impersonally. The subject is implied in the preceding words. So Cic. Att. iv. 8 b. 3 *audivi Romae esse hominem et fuisse adsiduum. Percussit animum.* The verb is often used of the emotions; but it should be noted that *percussus* sometimes has taken the place of *perculsus* by confusion in the MSS.

attat, ' ah !' Note the length of the last syllable.

hoc illud est. Cf. Verg. Aen. 4. 675 *hoc illud, germana, fuit.*

126. hinc illae lacrimae has become proverbial. Quoted by Cicero, Horace, and, in fact, by most people.

128. Note the dramatic change of tense throughout this passage.

131. ibi tum. Cf. 106 note.

exanimatus, ' distracted,' a common use of the word.

135. ut cerneres, 'so that you might have seen.' The mood is really independent of *ut*, and must be explained like that of *diceret* below. These potential subjunctives (as they are called rather unfortunately) simply form the apodosis of a conditional sentence, whose protasis is suppressed. Cf. Cic. de Fin. 2. 17 *poterat Sextilius impune negare; quis enim redargueret?* (i. e. *si negaret*). So *crederes, videres*, etc.

136. quam familiariter, ' with all a lover's trust ' (lit. ' how trustingly '). This is an exclamation added at the end of the sentence to strengthen the verb. So Eun. 178 *labascit victus uno verbo, quam*

cito, and Haut. 1023 *sed ipse egreditur, quam severus.* Sometimes we find *quam* strengthened by an adverb prefixed; e. g. *mire quam, sane quam.* Cf. θαυμαστῶς ὡς. The phrase can hardly be explained as = *quam potuit familiariter*, for this use of *quam* and the positive adjective or adverb is hardly found till after the Augustine period. Cf., however, Caes. B. G. 6. 26 *rami quam late diffunduntur*.

137. **quid ais.** These words occur very often in Terence. They are used (1) as a request for information, when a remark has not been fully heard, cf. 184; (2) as an exclamation of surprise, when a remark has been heard, but seems scarcely credible, as here, cf. 301, 588, 933; (3) to introduce a new point in conversation, or to call any one's attention, like 'dis donc,' cf. 517, 575.

aegre ferens, without object expressed, as Adel. 143 *aegre pati*.

138. **ad obiurgandum causae**, cf. 150. Equivalent to the more regular *obiurgandi causa*, which we have in 158.

139. **quid commerui**, 'what fault have I committed?' We may say that *quid = quam noxiam* (Plaut. Trin. 28), or *quam culpam* (Phor. 206), or *quid mali* (Plaut. Aul. 728). *Commerere* is used regularly in a bad, as *promerere* in a good sense.

141. **honesta oratiost**, 'it is a fair plea.'

143. Fleckeisen is surely wrong (followed by Spengel and Meissner) in altering *dederit* of the MSS. to *dedit*. The indic. *tulit* is necessary, because it refers to a definite act in past time; but *qui dederit damnum* has only a hypothetical existence.

dederit damnum aut malum, 'committed damage or outrage.' Cf. Plaut. Trin. 219 *cum damno et malo*, where *damno* = 'fine,' injury to property, *malo* = punishment, injury to person. *Damnum* is a passive partic. of *dare*, as *alumnus*, etc.; but the repetition of the verb is merely accidental.

145. The colon may be placed after *facinus* or *comperisse*. In the former case *indignum facinus* is an exclamation standing alone, as Adel. 173. The *Or. Recta* would be, *indignum facinus, Simo! comperi Pamphilum*, etc.

147. **instat factum**, (sc. *esse*), 'he insists that it is the case.' This construction occurs Plaut. Merc. 242, and perhaps nowhere else. Though uncommon, it does not seem odd. Cicero, too, has acc. and infin. after the similar verb *urgere*.

148. **qui**, indefinite; cf. 6 note. It is grammatically possible to take *qui* as nom. masc. here, but many other passages make the construction certain. The word would generally disappear in translation into English, e.g. 'we part on such terms that he declines to consent to his daughter's marriage.'

149. **non tu ibi natum,** sc. *obiurgasti.*

151. In the next three lines Simo gives the excuses (apparently considered valid) which his son would advance. 'By determining that I must marry soon, you have limited my time for intrigue (*his rebus*); before long I shall have to obey the whims of a wife (*alieno more*); let me have my fling now and sow my wild oats.'

praescripsti = *praescripsisti.* This syncopated form (*is* being omitted) of verbs, whose perf. indic. ends in -*si*, is used by Latin poets (1) in the second pers. sing. perf. indic. (often) and second pers. plur. (rarely); (2) in perf. infin.; (3) in pluperf. subj.; the sing. and first pers. plur. being found; but none of this last set in Terence. All the examples in this play are second pers. sing. perf. indic.; cf. 500, 506, 518, 572, 852, 882, 883: *iusse* occurs Haut. 1001, *produxe* Adel. 561, *decesse* Haut. 32. Vergil has *direxti, instruxti, traxe, extinxem, vixet,* and the rare *accestis.* See the exhaustive note of Klotz on this passage.

152. **prope adest quom,** 'the time is soon coming when.' Cf. Adel. 299, *nunc illud est quom.*

155. There are two doubtful points, on which it is impossible to pronounce positively: (1) A comma may be placed after *ducere*; then the apodosis is line 156; or a full stop, in which case the apodosis is line 154, and line 156 stands by itself; (2) *nolit* or *nolet*? On the whole we prefer the former, as having the MSS. authority; also cf. 165, 166, *sin eveniat—restat.*

amorem, i.e. for Glycerium.

156. 'This at length will be an act of disobedience on his part, which I must punish.'

primum, as elsewhere, almost = *demum.*

ab illo, closely with *iniuria.* Cf. Livy, 27. 2 *fides a consule.*

157-167. Simo now explains his *consilium* (line 50). 'I am going to tell Pamphilus that he must marry the daughter of Chremes, because (1) if he refuses, I shall have a definite ground for blaming him; (2) Davos always opposes my wishes, and I want him to waste his efforts in defeating an imaginary scheme; (3) if Pamphilus after all consents, I hope to talk Chremes over, and really bring about the marriage (165-167).

157. **id operam do.** Cf. 307. The neut. pron. is found after such verbs as *gaudere, studere, lacrumare,* where the accus. of a substantive could not stand. Cf. Madv. § 229. *id operam do* = *id ago,* and 58 note.

159. **sceleratus.** So Adel. 553 *eccum sceleratum Syrum.* The slave of Latin comedy is usually represented as opposing the wishes of his master, furthering the schemes of his master's son, and looking carefully after his own interests.

160. **consumat,** 'use it up.'

161. manibus pedibusque, Homer's χεροίν τε ποσίν τε. The phrase occurs again in 676 without *que*, which Bentley omits here also. If we accept the omission, it is possible (with Spengel) to extend the asyndeton to *obnixe*, and make *manibus, pedibus, obnixe* separately emphasise *facturum*. Indeed, as far as *sense* goes, *omnia* may make a fourth in the list.

162. id. Spengel supplies *facturum*. This is possible, but the run of the words is against such a construction, and there are other passages where the explanation is inadmissible. See especially 414 note. It is better to consider *id* an accus. of limitation, indicating the scope or object of the action, and further developed by *adeo ut incommodet*. 'Rather with this very object, that he may thwart my wishes.' Cf. Eun. 1005, *nunc id prodeo ut conveniam Parmenonem*.

adeo. Note the uses of *adeo*:

(1) 'so far,' (*a*) of space, Phor. 55 *res adeo redit;* (*b*) of time, 662; (*c*) of circumstance, 245.

(2) 'moreover,' 'besides.'

(3) *adeo ut*, 'for the purpose that,' as in this passage.

(4) intensive after (*a*) pronouns, 415, 579; (*b*) after adjectives or adverbs, 775; (*c*) after conjunctions, 440.

It is possible to take *adeo* as intensifying *id*, instead of joining it to *ut*.

164. mala mens, malus animus. Aristophanes, Pax, 1068 δόλιαι ψυχαί, δόλιαι φρένες. *Mens* and *animus*, 'mind and heart,' are often joined by Latin writers, probably without feeling the contrast very strongly.

165. sin eveniat. *sin*, as usual, in an alternative hypothesis; here contrasted with *si nolit* (155).

166. ut sit, epexegetic of *quod*.

167. confore, impersonal; this and *confuturum* are the only forms used. The rest of the verb is supplied by *confieri*.

171. nunciam, always three syllables in Plautus and Terence.

i prae, always in this order; cf. Adel. 167 *abi prae*. Wagner gives *eamus nunciam intro* to Simo, and *i prae, sequor* to Sosia, on the ground that the freedman would naturally follow his master; but the action of the play requires that Simo should remain on the stage, and must be responsible for any breach of etiquette.

ACT I. SCENE 2.

Simo meets Davos, and threatens him with penal servitude for life if he attempts to prevent the projected marriage.

173. modo, shortly before the conversation with Sosia.

175. mirabar, hoc si sic abiret, 'I always thought it wonderful if this conduct was really passing unnoticed,' *not*, 'whether it would pass,' etc.; i.e. *si abiret* is of course conditional, and *mirabar = mirum arbitrabar; hoc* and *sic*. vague words, explained by the position of affairs. For *sic abire*, cf. Cic. ad Att. 14. 1.

et eri, etc., 'and all through I feared to what my master's forbearance was tending.' It is possible to take *semper* closely with *lenitas*, 'constant forbearance.' a form of expression very common in Greek, and not unknown in Latin ; cf. Plaut. Pers. 385 *non tu nunc hominum mores vides*, where the construction seems certain. Further examples might be given, in Cicero, Livy, and Vergil, as well as Plautus and Terence ; but as there is no definite article to bind the phrase together, a different construction is almost always *possible*. In this passage the sense points to *semper verebar*. Davos was frightened by a special display of *lenitas* on a particular occasion, because he thought it to have been assumed by Simo in order to provoke no suspicion of his real intention. We must add that below (262) Pamphilus speaks of *lenis animus* as constantly characteristic of his father; but the experiences of son and slave may have been a little different.

178. The change from the iambic to the quicker trochaic metre gives liveliness and emphasis to the statement of the important fact. Simo naturally retorts in trochees. The same change for the same purpose recurs 182.

fecit = *dixit*, cf. 753.

179. **magno malo**, 'severe punishment.' Cf. 431, Plaut. Trin. 1062.

180. **sic**, explained by *necopinantes*.

duci = 'led on,' rather than 'misled.'

181. **oscitantis**, 'half asleep,' lit. 'yawning.'

183. **astute**, adverb.

carnufex, a common term of abuse addressed to slaves; cf. 651, 852; so *furcifer* (618), *mastigia*, and many others.

184. **ehodum**, cf. 29 note.

quid ais, 'what is it that you are saying?' Simo heard Davos speak, but did not distinguish the words.

185. **id populus curat scilicet**, 'of course the public is interested in his love affairs.' A sarcastic reference to Simo's statement that they were a matter of 'common talk.'

186. **hocine agis an non?** 'are you attending to my words or not?'

istuc = *quod dicis*.

ea. the past conduct of Pamphilus.

188. **ad eam rem tulit**, 'suited such conduct.' *tulit* is neuter, as in many phrases of the sort. Cf. 443, 832.

189. **hic dies**, i.e. of his wedding.

aliam—alios, 'different'—'different,' not 'one'—'other.'

190. dehinc, cf. 22 note.

sive = *vel si*. Cf. 293, 294.

in viam, 'into the right path.'

191. hoc quid sit? 'What is the point of all this?' Davos pretends not to understand how he is concerned with the conduct of Pamphilus. Simo proceeds to make it quite clear. The subjunctive must depend on an ellipse of some word like *quaero*. This construction is more common when one speaker quotes a question first asked by the other; e. g. 499, Adel. 84 *quid fecit?* to which Demea replies *quid ille fecerit?* (sc. *quaeris*). Accordingly some editors assign *hoc quid sit* to Simo. However, Davos has not asked, as he ought, *hoc quid est?* but he may have *looked* it.

qui amant, i. e. in love with some one other than the proposed *uxor*.

193. 'Too often he guides his heart, love-sick already, towards the worse object.' Cf. 924 *se adplicat*, a common phrase.

ipsum aegrotum must be taken together; = 'love-sick without the promptings of the *magister*.'

195. sane, a colloquial word for 'yes,' like *etiam*.

199. dedam usque ad necem, ' put you for the term of your natural life.'

200. ea lege atque omine, 'on the condition and solemn assurance that.' There is no parallel to this use of *omen*; but, as Mr. Papillon says, the idea of 'prognostic' may pass into that of 'warning.'

201. nondum etiam, an emphatic pleonasm, as *etiam* with a negative = *nondum*. Cf. 116 note.

callide = *plane*. We say, ' I *shrewdly* suspect.'

202. locutus possibly ought to be written *locutu's = locutus es*.

circuitione, five syllables, not six. As *circuiri* (Phor. 614) is four syllables, not three, and so *circuimus*, *circuit*, *circuis* used by Plautus, some editors write *circum itione* separately, so that the last syllable of *circum* may be elided. But this separation seems scarcely natural, and *circuitio* might be pronounced *circitio*.

203. passus sim. This potential subjunctive (cf. Mad. § 350 b, 135 note) is often used to express in a cautious way what will happen if certain circumstances arise. The perfect tense is usual, as here: 'I would sooner be deceived.' Cf. phrases like *haud facile dixerim*, 'I shall find it difficult to say.'

deludier, archaic form of the infin. pass., used also by poets generally.

204. bona verba, quaeso, 'hush, hush,' = εὐφήμει; cf. *favete linguis*. Davos pretends to be shocked to hear such an ill-omened word as *deludier* applied to his master.

205. **neque tu hoc dices,** etc., 'nor shall you say that you were not warned of this,' i. e. I speak so plainly, that you cannot mistake me. *Hoc*, given by the MSS., is altered by the editors into *haud* on the authority of Donatus, *neque haud* being understood like the Greek double negative. But (1) *hoc* gives a perfectly good sense, (2) Terence has no other instance of *neque haud*, though it is true that Plautus has, (3) Donatus says, '*tres negativae* [i.e. *neque, haud, non*] *pro una negativa accipiuntur*,' which clearly shows that he considered *neque* and *haud* not as strengthening, but as destroying each other; and that he objected to *hoc* because he thought a third negative necessary to the sense of the passage; in which view he will not find many followers.

Act I. Scene 3.

Davos, alone on the stage, reflects on the difficulties of the situation.

206. **enimvero;** cf. 91 note. Here, as there, it introduces a statement with emphasis.

208. **providentur,** 'prevented:' *providere* in this sense is regularly followed by the accusative, and it is impossible to understand why some editors explain *quae providentur* as irregular for *quibus providetur*, which would mean the exact opposite.

210. **eius,** like **illum,** refers to Pamphilus: *eius* and *huius* are monosyllables.

212. **nequam faciam,** etc., 'lest I should use any intrigue to defeat this intended match.'

213, 214. A passage of great difficulty. It seems best to explain the construction as follows:—*si senserit aut causam ceperit* is protasis; *quo—dabit* is apodosis; *perii* is merely a parenthetical exclamation, not connected with the construction of the sentence; *si lubitum fuerit* is a subordinate protasis, qualifying *causam*, equal in sense to *quam lubitum fuerit* (*capere*). Bentley goes so far as to read *quam* instead of *si*. Translate, 'If he actually detects me, (ruin!) or even finds a pretext satisfactory to himself, rightly or wrongly he will hurry me off to the mill.' The remaining difficulty belongs to *quo iure quaque iniuria*, which is equivalent in sense to καὶ δικαίως κἀδίκως (Aristoph. Plut. 233); but it seems hopeless to attempt any explanation of the relatives as the passage stands, unless Terence supposed himself to be translating ὡς δικαίως κἀδίκως or something of the sort. Bentley's emendation *qua iure qua me iniuria*, (*qua—qua=cum—tum* as elsewhere), is at any rate translateable. It is usual to take *perii* and *ceperit* as apodosis, and *quo—dabit* as a relative clause, 'if he detects me, *perii*; if he takes the fancy, he will find a reason for sending me to the mill,' a rendering objectionable (among other reasons) because it contrasts '*perishing*' with being sent to the *pistrinum*. What Davos feared in any case was not execution, but hard labour.

218. **amentium, haud amantium**, an excellent instance of the play upon words (paronomasia), so much affected by Plautus, but rare in Terence.

219. **quidquid**, neuter gender, because the sex is uncertain.

peperisset, oblique for *pepererit* (cf. 3 note).

decreverunt is historic.

tollere, 'acknowledge.' The father formally acknowledged the newly-born child, and undertook to bring it up as his own, by raising it from the ground, when it had been laid before him: *suscipere* also is used in this sense; cf. 401.

220. **fallaciam**, 'absurd story.' Note the mixture of *oratio recta* and *obliqua* in the following lines. The story is true, as we afterwards discover; but Davos of course does not know that it is.

223. **ibi tum**. Cf. 106 note.

225. **atque**. For the adversative sense, cf. 607.

226. **ab ea** = *a Glycerio*, i.e. from the house of Glycerium. Cf. 461, 682. This use of the person for the house is common in Terence.

me, sc. *conferam*. Cf. 361.

227. **opprimat**, 'surprise.'

ACT I. SCENE 4.

Mysis, maid to Glycerium, enters from the house, and standing by the door continues a conversation with Archilis, who remains within.

231. **tamen**, i.e. notwithstanding her drunkenness and carelessness. After *adducam* Archilis is supposed to reply from within, 'Yes, you must bring her.' This provokes Mysis to speak of her *inportunitas*, 'obstinacy.'

aniculae, diminutive to express contempt.

232. **compotrix**, ἅπαξ λεγ. in classical Latin.

233. **aliis**, sc. *mulieribus*.

peccandi, 'bungling.'

234. **siet**. All the sing. and the third plur. of this form are used by Terence and Plautus. Cf. 586, *siem*; 408, 424, *sies*; 454, *siet*; 288, 390, *sient*.

235. **numquidnam**, used by Terence as indirect as well as direct interrogative.

turba, 'confusion,' visible in the appearance of Pamphilus.

tristitiae, genitive after *numquidnam*.

Act I. Scene 5.

Pamphilus complains bitterly of the attempts made by Simo and Chremes to force a wife upon him, protests that he will never leave Glycerium, and describes how Chrysis on her death-bed committed her to his charge. Mysis remains in the background till 267.

The mixture of Iambic and Trochaic lines in this scene suits well the expression of strong feeling.

236. **hocinest**, etc. 'Is this the act or purpose of a human being? is this the duty of a father?' The argument is, 'if any one of human feeling *cannot* do this, how absurd to say that a father *ought* to do it!' If *-ne* is added to *hice, haece, hoce*, the final *e* in these words is changed into *i*. For *factum* and *inceptum* some read *factu* and *inceptu*. It seems to be a matter of speculation; in such a case MSS. do not help us much, as the final *m* is indicated merely by a mark over the *u*.

237. **fidem**, sc. *imploro*. Cf. 246, 716 *di vostram fidem*. *Pro* does not affect the case of the word to which it is joined, as may be seen from such phrases as *pro supreme Iuppiter, pro di immortales*.

deum is a monosyllable.

Note **quid ĕst si haéc**; *quid est*, sc. *contumelia*.

238. **dare sese.** The common construction after *decerno, constituo*, etc. is the pres. infin. without a subject.

nonne. It is doubtful whether we ought not to read *non* here and in the next line. Plautus and Terence ordinarily use *-ne* or *non* instead of *nonne*. Cf. 17 note.

239. **praescisse ante.** Note the pleonasm.

Of **oportuit** Donatus says *quam de stomacho repetitum est*.

242. **suam uxorem.** We may scan *suam* as a monosyllable and elide both vowels, or, considering it as a dissyllable, shorten the first syllable of *uxorem*.

id, 'his purpose.'

inmutatum. If this word is the pass. participle of *inmutare* (cf. 275), it must mean 'changed,' as *in* has no negative force in composition with verbs. Spengel takes it thus, explaining that Pamphilus' grief at the idea of marriage had changed into joy when he found that Chremes refused to allow the match. It is much better to consider it as an adjective, 'unchanged.' The remark is intelligible enough, though not quite logical. Pamphilus, contrasting the changed purpose of Chremes with his own unchangeable fidelity, speaks as if the one were the consequence of the other.

244. si fit, pereo, a graphic variety for *si fiet, peribo*.

245. 'Can any man be so hapless in love or so unfortunate as I am?' This use of the acc. and infin. in indignant exclamations (mostly introduced by the interrogative *-ne*) is very common. Surprise at the existence of some state of things is combined with a question whether such can really be the case. Cf. 253, 425, 609, 689, 870, 879.

invenustus = ἀναφρόδιτος. Join *adeo ut ego sum*. Cf. 162 note.

247. Chremetis. Like some other Greek proper names this word follows more than one form of inflexion. Cf. *Chremetem* 472, 533, *Chremeti* Phor. 1026; but *Chremi* (genitive) 368, *Chremem* 361, 527. As for the vocative, there is plenty of MSS. authority both for *Chremes* and *Chreme*.

248. quot modis. We do not hear of any attempts on the part of Simo to induce Chremes to give his consent, after the match was once broken off. The reference probably is to a number of strong expressions used by Chremes, which would lose nothing in transmission through Simo to Pamphilus.

facta transacta, 'settled and concluded,' i. e. the match was definitely 'off.' For the asyndeton in this line, cf. 304, 373.

249. nisi si, like *quasi si*, εἰ μή εἰ, πλὴν ἐάν, the hypothetical force of the first word being forgotten. Cf. Adel. 594, Plaut. Trin. 474.

250. aliquid monstri. Cf. 2 note, *id negoti*.

alunt, like a beast. Cf. 57.

ea, gender accommodated to sense. Cf. 607.

252. nam. The connexion seems to be : 'I try to explain the conduct of Chremes ; for how can I explain that of my father?'

253. Cf. 245 note.

254. apud forum = *in foro*, as often in Plautus and Terence. Cf. 302, 745.

para, absolute.

257. causam, 'excuse.'

258-9. 'Now if any one asked me, what I should have done if I had been forewarned of it, (I should answer), I would have done something to escape from doing this.' The apodosis to *si quis roget* must be supplied ; the primary tense is used because the supposition is possible. On the other hand, *si rescissem facerem* contains an impossible hypothesis.

ut ne = *ne*, as often. Cf. 699, and 335 *qui ne*.

quod si, not found in Plautus, rare in Terence common later. Cf. 604. *Quod* is properly an accusative of limitation ; cf. 289.

261. huius, 'for her,' i. e. Glycerium ; objective, as *patris* in the next line.

G

nuptiarum, with the daughter of Chremes.

263. quae—quomque. Cf. 63 note.

eĭne ego ut advorser? 'can I oppose *him*'? Note the emphatic position of *ei*. Mad. (§ 353 obs.) explains this construction as =*fierine potest ut* etc., and it is clear that there must be an ellipse of something of the sort. Cf. 618, where the interrogative -*ne* is omitted.

264. quorsum accidat. 'what will be the end' of this hesitation? Cf. 127, 176. Mysis is afraid that the 'hesitation' of Pamphilus will end in the desertion of Glycerium. Some alter *incertum* to *incertumst* to avoid the hiatus, which, however, is sufficiently accounted for by the isolated position of *incertum*. It is a further question, whether the hiatus should be admitted between *timeo* and *incertum* or *incertum* and *hoc*. We follow Klotz in preferring the latter.

265. peropus, ἅπαξ λεγ. Terence has a large number of adjectives and adverbs compounded with *per*.

ipsa, Glycerium.

advorsum hunc = *coram hoc*. In 42 *advorsum te = tibi*.

266. paulo momento, 'by a slight impulse.' *Paulus* is used as an adjective by Terence here and Adel. 876. In later Latin we find the neut. *paulum* and the comparative adv. *paulo*.

267. Pamphile. Cf. 23 *dicere* and note.

268. dolore, pains of child-birth; in this sense usually plural.

269. nuptiae, of Pamphilus with the daughter of Chremes.

272-3. 'Who trusted me with her heart, even with her life, while I have made her the darling of my heart, and loved her with a husband's love.' The change from indicative to subjunctive is noticeable, but gives no difficulty: *quae—credidit* merely states the fact; *quam —habuerim* states the reason on account of which Pamphilus thought it impossible to desert her. Terence might have written otherwise, i. e. *crediderit— habui*, or two indicatives or two subjunctives. In a case like this a change of mood merely indicates a change in the point of view from which the speaker regards the proposition. If, as here, that change in the point of view is intelligible, the grammatical explanation is equally simple. For a mixture of moods, cf. 536, 650, notes.

274. bene et pudice doctum atque eductum, 'taught and trained in virtue and purity.'

275. ingenium, 'character.'

277. sed vim ut queas ferre, 'but (I fear) that you may be unable to resist compulsion.'

279, 280. The substantives in 280 answer to the adjectives in 279 with the order inverted. If a man is not *ferus*, he is influenced by *consuetudo* at any rate; if not *inhumanus* (going a step higher), by *amor*; if not *ingratus* (higher still), by *pudor*. Tr., 'So unfeeling, so inhuman, so unnatural, that neither association (which influences even the brute creation), nor love (which influences all *men*), nor honour (which influences all men of feeling) stir me and admonish me to keep my pledge.' Note the intensive force of *con*. Cf. Plaut. Trin. 26 *concastigabo pro conmerita noxia*, after *castigare* and *meritam* have been used.

282. memor essem, an echo of *memor esses;* hence the tense and mood. Cf. 649.

283. scripta, predicate.

285. vos, you and the other attendant women.

287. nec clam te est = *nec te fugit*.

utraeque. An irregular use of the plural, since two objects, not two sets of objects, are meant. However, it is not uncommon; several instances are given from prose writers. The reading res nunc utiles (Fleckeisen following Bentley) is unnatural, as giving an ironical sense to *utiles*, quite out of keeping with the rest of the passage. Contrast 811. It was suggested by the appearance of *res* (evidently a gloss) in some MSS. and the remark of Donatus, '*legitur et utiles*.'

288. sient. Cf. 234 note.

289. The arrangement of this line is rather doubtful, but it is only necessary to note that *genium*, given by Donatus, is preferable to *ingenium* of MSS.

quod (accus. of respect, cf. 738, 258 *quod si*) = 'whereas,' and is a common introduction to invocations.

genium tuom, 'your own self.' Cf. Hor. Ep. 1. 7. 94 *quod te per genium dextramque deosque Penates Obsecro et obtestor*, and Mr. Macleane's note: 'The Romans believed that every man had a genius, though their notions on the subject were very confused apparently. According to the name it should be the attendant on a man's birth, as it was believed to be the inseparable companion of his life. It represented his spiritual identity, and the character of the genius was the character of the man. . . . . This explains the expressions *genio indulgere*, etc.'

293, 294. sive—seu. Each = *vel si*. Cf. 190.

295. virum, 'husband.'

296. fide. This form of the genitive and dative is common in Plautus, less frequent in Terence; found sometimes in later authors.

300. cave, sc. dicas.

hoc, sc. *accedat*.

teneo, 'I understand.' Cf. 349, 498.

Act II. Scene 1.

Charinus, who is in love with Philumena, daughter of Chremes, hears from his slave Byrria of her proposed marriage with Pamphilus. The latter, being entreated by Charinus to postpone the match, professes the greatest readiness to do so.

301. **quid ais.** An expression of surprise; cf. 137. It is provoked by some words spoken by Byrria before the opening of the scene. We must scan *datŭrne*, if the final vowel of *Byrria* is long, as seems probable. Cf. *Chaereā*, Eun. 558.

302. **qui**, interrogative. Cf. 6 note.

apŭd forum = *in foro*. Cf. 254.

ei. Fleckeisen's emendation for *vae*, which avoids the shortening of *e*.

303. **usque** = *semper*.

attentus, 'on the strain.'

304. **cura**, with *confectus*, not with *lassus*, as the alliteration shows. Tr., 'wearied and worn with care, it is paralysed.'

305. **edepol**, 'by Pollux,' like the shorter form *pol*, is very common in Plautus and Terence. Cf. 486 *ecastor*.

306. **id velis**, etc., i.e. 'marry somebody else.'

Philumenam, evidently spoken emphatically, with reference to the meaning of the name, which of course = ἡ φιλουμένη.

307. **id dare operam.** Cf. 157 note.

qui. Cf. 6 note.

309. A commonplace in Greek; cf. Aesch. Prom. 263, Soph. Trach. 729, Eur. Alc. 1078, and a line quoted by Muretus, ὑγιὴς νοσοῦντα ῥᾷστα πᾶς τις νουθετεῖ.

310. **hic** = *ego*, like Greek ὅδε ἀνήρ. Cf. 890, Plaut. Trin. 1115. He says it δεικτικῶς, with a gesture, pointing at himself.

si sis, sentias. The use of the pres. subj. has the rhetorical effect of representing the supposition as possible. Cf. 914, Mad. § 347 obs.

age, age, ut lubet, 'well, well, as you like.' Byrria, finding that his philosophic remarks are without effect, gives up Charinus as hopeless. So Phor. 662 *age, age, iam ducat, dabo*.

311. **prius quam pereo.** The stricter syntax of later Latin would require *peream*, as these words express the *purpose* of the speaker; but by using the indicative, which makes the idea of simple *time* predominant, Charinus emphasises the hopelessness of his position.

hic, Charinus.

313. **credo**, parenthetical; cf. 673. So too 314 *spero*, 578 *censes*,

854 *faxo* (but see note). Cicero is very fond of using *credo* thus in an ironical sense.

prodat, 'prolong,' 'lengthen out,' some days for the marriage; i. e. 'let some few days elapse before the marriage.' For this use of *prodo* in the sense of *produco* (615) cf. Plaut. Trin. 340 *illi prodit vitam ad miseriam*.

315. **adeon**, 'am I to go to him?' For this emphatic use of the pres. indic. instead of the future or the deliberative subjunct., cf. Verg. Aen. 3. 88 *quem sequimur?*

320. **ad auxilium copiam** = *auxili copiam*. Cf. 138 note.

321. **istuc**, 'your request.'

322. **postremum**, 'for the last time.'

324. **ne**, 'really': only used with pronouns and their adverbs. Cf. 772.

327. **principio** = μάλιστα μέν; answered by *saltem* in the next line.
ut ne = *ne*. Cf. 259.

si id non potest = '*s'il ne se peut*.' Terence often has *potest* impersonally, or with a neut. pronoun for subject. Cf. Phor. 227, 303, 818. See below, 861 note.

328. **haec** (for *haece*) is the regular form of the fem. plur. in Plautus and Terence; probably it remained in use even later. Cf. 438, 656. But the MSS. often give *hae*.

329. **profer**. Either (1) sc. *nuptiis*, 'prolong some few days for the marriage,' or (2) sc. *nuptias*, ' put off the marriage for some few days,' taking *dies* as acc. of time, not as the object. The first gives an unusual sense to *proferre*, but the striking parallel in 313 is almost decisive in its favour.

dum proficiscor. We might expect the subjunctive, as the idea of purpose, not of time, is prominent. But after verbs of 'waiting' and suchlike *dum* and the indic. is found even in Cicero. Cf. Cic. Att. x. 3 *ego in Arcano opperior, dum haec cognosco*; and often in Terence; cf. 714, Phor. 982 *retine dum ego huc servos evoco*, Haut. 833. Notice that such a translation as 'while I am going' disguises and does not explain the difficulty. The idea of purpose will still be the prominent idea.

330. **ne utiquam**. Always two words in Plautus and Terence, for the vowel of *ne* must be elided if the first syllable is short; and this is usually proved by the metre. It is true that *neutiquam* is possible (not necessary), Hec. 403.

liberi hominis, as we might say, ' of a gentleman.'

331. **id**, 'his act.'

gratiae adponi, 'counted as a favour'; lit. 'be set down to favour'; cf. Hor. Od. 1. 9. 14 *lucro adpone*.

sibi, 'to his credit;' *dat. commodi.*

332. **apiscier**. The simple verb is probably usual in Plautus and Terence, though it has often been altered in MSS. (especially the later) to *adipisci*. The latter, however, is proved by the metre, Phor. 412.

334. **qui**. Cf. 6 note. So in the next line, *qui ne = ut ne.*

335. **sat habeo**, 'I am satisfied.' Cf. 705, 710.

optume = *opportune.* Cf. 686.

336. **quicquam**, sc. *dicis.* Cf. 82.

337. **nisi ea quae nil opus sunt scire**, 'except the knowledge of those things, which are useless.' *Ea* is object after *scire*. Charinus is referring to Byrria's commonplace remarks, e. g. 305. Bentley changed *scire* (given by all MSS.) into *sciri*, on the ground that otherwise *est* must be read for *sunt*, and he has been followed by most editors, who, of course, take *sciri* as epexegetic of *opus sunt*, as Bentley did.

fugin hinc, colloquial for the imperative, 'be off.'

ego vero ac lubens = *ego vero fugio ac lubens fugio: ac* = ' and indeed;' emphatic. Cf. 370.

ACT II. SCENE 2.

Davos informs Charinus and Pamphilus that Simo's announcement of the marriage is not seriously meant, and describes the observations which led him to this conclusion.

338. **boni, boni**. For similar repetitions of a word, cf. 947, 958.

340. **laetus est nescio quid**. Cf. Adel. 79 *nescio quid tristem video.*

342. **audin tu illum**. Davos' last words show that he has heard of the marriage. Therefore Charinus points out that Pamphilus is wrong in saying *nondum haec rescivit mala.*

343. **intendam**, sc. *gradus* or *iter.*

344. **abeo**, given by all MSS., for which Donatus has *habeo*, 'I have it,' 'I know,' = *inveni*. If *habeo* is accepted, Davos means that after all —notwithstanding *toto me oppido exanimatum quaerere*— Glycerium's house is the most likely place.

resiste, 'stop.'

qui me, sc. *revocat* or something of the sort.

345. **euge**. The last syllable is short, Greek εὖγε. It is quite unnecessary to insert *o* before *Charine*, for the pause after *quaero* justifies the hiatus.

ambo, sc. *adestis.*

vos volo. Cf. 29.

346. **quin audi**. Cf. 45 note.

347. **quid tu**, sc. *timeas.*

348. **etsi scio?** sc. something like *tamen pergis dicere?* answering to *obtundis*, but milder.

hodie, sc. *sunt paratae.*

349. **tenes.** Cf. 300.

350. **istuc ipsum**, 'the very point.' Probably acc. in apposition to *rem.*

me vide, 'look to me,' 'trust to me.' Cf. Phor. 711, Plaut. Trin. 808.

352. **non iam**, 'no longer.' Emphatic; the danger is over.

qui. Cf. 6 note.

354. Some MSS. give *sese* at the beginning of this line; but (1) it creates a metrical difficulty; (2) it is very likely to have been written originally as a marginal note, and thence to have crept into the text; (3) Terence constantly omits the subject of the infinitive. Cf. 14 note.

alia multa, e.g. threats of punishment. Cf. 196 foll.

356. **ibi**, 'then.' Cf. 106 note. But in the next line it is probably local.

357. **huius**, 'slave to Charinus here.' Genitive of possession. So Verg. Aen. 3. 319 *Hectoris Andromache.*

359. **redeunti**, i.e. to the house of Simo.

ex ipsa re, 'from the state of things,' without any information.

360. **paululum**, used by Terence both as a substantive and an adjective.

ipsus, 'my master,' common for *ipse* in Plautus and Terence. Cf. 495, 576, 598, etc.

tristis, 'out of temper.'

361. **non cohaerent**, i.e. the three things mentioned in the previous line are inconsistent. A marriage ought to have produced festivity and good humour.

istuc, sc. *narras* or *evadit.*

me, sc. *confero.*

362. **illo**, adv. = *illuc.*

id gaudeo. Cf. 157 note.

363. **recte dicis**, like 970 *narras probe*, of good news.

364. **matronam**, the *pronuba*, whose duty it was to dress the bride, conduct her to her husband's house, etc.

365. **ornati, tumulti.** The following genitives in *-i* for *-us* are found in Terence, *domi, quaesti, tumulti, fructi, ornati, adventi,* and in Plautus, *domi, quaesti, tumulti, victi, senati, sumpti, gemiti.* Note especially that neither ever has *domus* for the genitive. The old form was *-uis*; cf. Haut. 287 *annis*, Phor. 482 *metuis*. The form in *-us* is

a simple contraction of this; the form in -*i* is a contraction after the lightly pronounced -*s* had been allowed to drop.

368. **Chremi.** Cf. 247 note.

369. The line in Menander's Perinthia, from which this was copied, runs, τὸ παιδίον δ' εἰσῆλθεν ἑψητοὺς φέρον.

ferre, histor. infin., which seems harsh here, notwithstanding Terence's fondness for it. Cf. 62 note. But the only alternative is to consider *conveni* as = *venire vidi*, and to take *ferre* as continuing the construction κατὰ ξύνεσιν. If MSS. counted for nothing at all, Bentley's correction *conspexi* might be allowed to solve the difficulty.

obolo, abl. of price.

in cenam, 'for dinner,' a use of *in* and acc. to express purpose not found in good prose. But cf. Plaut. Mil. 3. 2. 19 *in prandium*.

370. **ac.** Cf. 337 note.

nullus = an emphatic *non* sometimes in Plautus and Terence. Cf. Plaut. Trin. 606 *nullus creduas*. Here sc. *liberatus es*.

371. **ridiculum caput.** Cf. Adel. 261 *festivom caput*. So κάρα is used. We say 'blockhead,' etc.

372. **necessus.** Here the MSS. give *necesse*, for which Lachmann (on Lucretius 6. 815) restored *necessus*, as being the form always used by Terence before consonants. It is given by the Bembine MS. Eun. 998, Haut. 360, in both cases before a consonant; and there is little doubt that it would have appeared here too, if that MS. had not unfortunately been mutilated. It begins at 786.

si huic non dat, 'inasmuch as he does not give her to Pamphilus.' Note the indic.

si = *siquidem*.

373. **nisi vides**, 'unless indeed you look to it:' *nisi* must be explained by the ellipse of something like *neque quidquam efficies*.

ambis, 'canvass.' For the asyndeton cf. 248, 304.

ACT II. SCENE 3.

Davos urges Pamphilus to profess obedience to his father's wish that he should marry Philumena, on the ground that he can do so safely, since Chremes will persist in refusing his consent. With some misgiving Pamphilus promises to take his advice.

375. **igitur**, i.e. if the marriage is not seriously meant.

376. **id**, accus. of respect. Cf. 448. It is here explained by the clause which follows.

det, subjunctive, because not the fact, but the effect upon Simo's mind, is important. Of course Pamphilus, not Chremes, is the person with whom Simo will be principally angry; but 'anger at the refusal of Chremes' (which Terence actually writes) is much the same thing as 'anger with Pamphilus for causing the refusal.'

377. **tuom ut sese habeat animum** = *ut tuos animus sese habeat*, an imitation of Greek.

378. Note the assonance **iniurius—iniuria**. *Neque id iniuria*, 'and that rightly.' Cf. 60.

379. **negaris ducere** = *negaris te ducturum esse*. For a still more striking instance cf. 411; also 613. The continuative force of the present makes it almost equivalent to a future.

ibi, of time.

380. **illae turbae**, 'the dreaded explosion' of the wrath of Simo.

381. **difficilest**, sc. *resistere ei*.

tum, introducing a new ground, as in 192. It follows *ibi* (379), not of course *tum* (380).

dictum ac factum, or **dictum factum** (Haut. 904) = ἅμ' ἔπος ἅμ' ἔργον, 'no sooner said than done,' not quite so strong as *dicto citius*, but used with just the same effect.

382. **eiciat**, sc. Glycerium.

384. **ne nega**. For *ne* and imperative, which became very uncommon in later Latin, cf. 543, 868.

385. **ex ea re**, i.e. from following my advice.

386. **ut ab illa excludar, huc concludar**, 'to be shut off from her (Glycerium), I am to be shut up here!' (in the house of Chremes with Philumena). An angry explanation of the '*quid fiat*' of Davos. Pamphilus means, 'this will be the result of following your advice.' *Concludar* implies 'caged' like a wild beast. Cf. Phor. 744 *conclusam hic habeo uxorem saevam*.

387–398. Davos argues thus: 'You must tell your father, that you will marry Philumena, if he wishes it. Thereby you will leave him no just cause for blaming you, and will upset his plans, which are formed on the supposition that you will refuse; meantime he will not find you another match at once, and something may turn up in your favour. In acting thus you incur no risk, for Chremes is sure to persist in withholding his consent, especially if you keep up your relations with Glycerium. In fact you will gain the credit of complying with your father's wishes without any danger of those wishes being carried out. Perhaps you think, 'I can boldly meet my father with a refusal; all that he can do is to try to marry me to *some one*, and he will find no one who wants a man like me for a son-in-law. But I warn you that he will rather marry you to some penniless girl (whose parents will not be too particular), than allow you to entangle yourself with a stranger like Glycerium.' This scheme sounded plausible enough; Chremes spoilt it by consenting to the match after all.

389. **hic**, 'thereupon;' like *ibi*, of time. Spengel stops after *hic*, which he takes as = *pater* with *iurgabit;* but the adverb is quite necessary to *reddes*.

390. **ei**, like ea (392), is monosyllable.

ut sient must be regarded as an afterthought, since its addition to the phrase strictly requires *facies* instead of *reddes*; i.e. we should expect either *reddes omnia consilia incerta* or *facies omnia consilia incerta ut sient*.

391. **sine ŏmni** = *sine ullo*. Cf. Plaut. Trin. 338 *sine omni malitia*. Not in other writers.

392–393. **nec tu ea**, etc., 'but do not on that account alter your present conduct (i. e. your intrigue with Glycerium), lest he should change his determination' (i. e. give you his daughter after all). Davos means, 'however determined Chremes is now, we must run no unnecessary risks.' But it is possible to take the passage differently. 'And do not alter your present conduct (i. e. your professed compliance with your father's wishes), merely from fear that (*ea causa ne*) he may change his determination.' In other words, 'There is no danger in compliance; you can trust the obstinacy of Chremes.' Here *ne mutet* depends on *ea causa*, not, as in the first case, on *minueris*. The vagueness of *haec quae facis*, and perhaps the present tense, are in favour of the former rendering.

minuere = *mutare*. Cf. Hec. 616 *sed non minuam meum consilium*.

395–396. **nam quod tu**, etc., 'for though you may hope, "I shall easily repel a wife by a character like mine, no parent will give one to me." (I tell you that) he will find some dowerless maiden rather than allow you to be ruined.' *speres*, concessive subjunctive. *propulsabo*, a military metaphor; the bad character of Pamphilus is the weapon with which he repels the enemy. This passage is taken differently by putting a stop after *facile* and after *nemo*: 'I shall easily dispose of your hope, "No one will give a wife to a man of my character;" he will find, &c.' But this gives a very unnatural sense to *propulsabo*; and *his moribus* for *homini sic morato* is odd.

399. **vide**, 'consider.'

quin taces. Cf. 45 note.

400. **dicam**, sc. *me ducturum esse*.

puerum, 'child;' the sex was at present uncertain.

cautiost=*cavendum est.* Cf. Adel. 421.
401. suscepturum. Cf. 219 *tollere.*
402. qui = *ut.*

Act II. Scene 4.

Davos urges Pamphilus to meet his father boldly.

404. reviso = *redeo ut videam.* Donatus. Simo acts as he had instructed Sosia; cf. 170.

406. meditatus, often used of 'getting up' a part. Cf. Plaut. Trin. 817 *meditatum probe mittam,* Adel. 195.

408. qui, abl., as in 6.

    differat, 'confound,' lit. 'tear in pieces.'

    proin tu fac apud te ut sies, 'accordingly take care to keep your presence of mind.' *proin* monosyllable, as always.

409. modo ut possim, sc. *apud me ero: modo ut = dummodo.* See Mad. § 351 b. Obs. 2.

410. commutaturum. In the same sense Phor. 638 *tria non commutabitis verba hodie inter vos.*

411. verbum, i. e. of blame.

    ducere. Cf. 379 note.

Act II. Scene 5.

Byrria hears Pamphilus, prompted by Davos, promise to marry Philumena.

412. erus, sc. Charinus.

414. id, 'therefore;' cf. 162 note. Here it is emphasised and repeated by *propterea.*

    hunc, Simo, who has just entered. Byrria knows that, if Pamphilus goes wrong, it will be in Simo's company. Therefore to watch the one is as good as to watch the other.

415. ipsum, Pamphilus.

    adeo, emphasises *ipsum.* Cf. 162 note.

    hoc agam, 'I will attend to this,' i.e. their conversation. Cf. 186.

416. serva, 'remember,' sc. *mea praecepta,* or something of the sort.

417. quasi de improviso, 'as if you did not expect him,' i. e. innocently, naturally.

419. nostrae parti and quid hic respondeat both follow *timeo.*

421. obmutuit, sc. Simo, who, as Davos had foretold (390, 410), was not at all prepared for obedience.

422. 'When my request is granted with a good grace.' In later Latin we should find *impetrem*, the logical connexion being prominent, not, as here, the connexion of time.

423. **sum verus**, 'Am I not a true prophet?' This refers to 410, 411. Here *verus* = *veridicus*. Cf. Plaut. Mil. 1369, where it is opposed to *mendax*.

erus uxore excidit, 'my master has lost his wife.' The expression is rather odd; but cf. Plaut. Men. 667 *ex hac familia me plane excidisse intellego*. Ἐκπίπτειν is used of fall from power, disappointment of hopes, &c.

424. **in mora sies**, 'keep us waiting;' cf. 467. *Sies*, cf. 234, &c.

425. **esse**. Cf. 253 note.

426. **verbum**, 'saying.'

427. 'All wish to be better off than their fellow.' The double comparative *malle melius* is noticeable. For the sentiment cf. Eur. Med. 86 ὡς πᾶς τις αὑτὸν τοῦ πέλας μᾶλλον φιλεῖ, and a fragment of Menander, φιλεῖ δ' ἑαυτοῦ πλεῖον οὐδεὶς οὐδένα.

431. **ut pro hoc malo mihi det malum**. 'that for my sorry news he may give me sorry wages.' For this common use of *malum* in the sense of 'punishment,' cf. 179; and for the play on the two senses of the word, cf. Plaut. Trin. 554, 555, St. *quamvis malam rem quaeras, illic reperias*. Ph. *at tu hercle et illi et alibi*.

Act II. Scene 6.

Davos assures Simo, who is not without suspicion of deceit, that Pamphilus is sincere in his professed readiness to marry Philumena.

433. **ea gratia** = *eius rei gratia*. Cf. 587.

434. **aeque quicquam nunc quidem**, 'nothing now, just as before.' The use of *quicquam*, suggesting a negative, shows that *quicquam nunc quidem* = *ne nunc quidem quicquam*; and *aeque* = *aeque atque antea*. Davos means, 'I have no more to say than I had at our last interview.' Cf. 194. All through this dialogue he is thinking of his conversation with Simo, Act I, Scene 2.

436. **male habet**, 'troubles.' Cf. 940.

437. **dicere**. The final syllable must be long here; but cf. 23 note.

438. **quidpiam**, 'in any way.'

haec. Cf. 328.

439. 'On account of his association with this strange woman.'

440. **si adeo**, 'if really' (sc. *haec nuptiae illi molestae sunt*). For the force of *adeo* cf. 415, 162 note.

442. via, 'aright,' a remembrance of Simo's ironical request (190) that Pamphilus *iam redeat in viam*. *Recta*, which has got into the MSS. against the metre, must be a gloss on *via*, due to some one who did not see that the word has much more point without the adjective.

443. ei, a spondee, as Haut. 455 and always in Lucretius.
    dumque aetas tulit. Cf. 188.

445. fortem, of character, 'estimable.' Cf. Phor. 324 *O vir fortis atque amicus*.

446. animum adpulit. Cf. 1 note.

448. quod, accus. of respect or limitation. Cf. 376.

449. quin die, quid est. Cf. 45 note.

451. drachumis. The old form from δραχμή was *drachuma*, as Alcumena from Ἀλκμήνη, etc.

    obsonatum, passive impersonal, but perhaps *obsonatus* from deponent *obsonari* ought to be read.

454. quod dicendum hic siet, 'as far as one in my place may speak:' *hic*, 'by me to you,' though it may = 'between ourselves,' i.e. in the absence of Pamphilus: *siet*, cf. 234. The subjunctive is here used in the relative clause to express 'humiliation.' Cf. Mad. § 364, obs. 2, and such expressions as *quod sciam, quod meminerim*.

455. quoque, 'in fact;' for the meaning is not, 'You like others are stingy,' but, 'it is true, as well as declared by Pamphilus, that you are stingy.'

    per parce nimium. Tmesis for *pernimium parce*. Cf. 486. It is possible, however, that we should read *perparce*.

    non laudo. A comic repetition of Simo's *laudo* in 443.

457. rei, monosyllable here and in the next line.
    veterator, 'old rascal.'

ACT III. SCENE 1.

Simo overhears a conversation about Glycerium and her child. He thinks that the story has been invented by Davos to prevent Chremes from allowing the marriage between Pamphilus and Philumena.

459. pol, a common abbreviation for *edepol*.

460. invenias, potential subjunctive. Cf. 53, 135 etc.

461. ab Andria, 'from the Andrian's house.' Cf. 226 note.
    narras = *dicis*, as often in Terence.

464. Cf. 219.

465. actumst, 'it is all over,' an expression used originally in the law-courts of a case already concluded. So Phor. 419 '*actum*,' *aiunt, ne agas*.

sīquidem is found in Ovid also with the first syllable short. Here Spengel reads *si equidem*.

467. **in mora illi sis.** Cf. 424.

471. **adfertur fallacia.** Cf. 432 *fallaciam portare*.

474. **cito.** The pause helps to lengthen the last syllable. Terence has it short, when the word is not followed by a pause. Cf. Adel. 443.

475. **non sat commode divisa sunt temporibus tibi, Dave, haec**, 'your incidents, Davos, are not skilfully timed.' Simo might have said that they were too skilfully timed. They happened so exactly as they were wanted, that they looked artificial.

477. **num immemores discipuli**, 'have your pupils really forgotten their lesson?' *Num* has an ironical force: *discipuli*, though masculine, refers to Mysis, Lesbia, and Glycerium.

479. **quos mihi ludos redderet**, 'what tricks he would have played upon me!' *Now* Simo does not mind, because he is *paratus*, and the marriage is not *verae*.

480. **ego in portu navigo**, proverbial for 'I am safe.' Cf. 845 *omnis res est iam in vado*. So ἐν λιμένι πλέω.

Act III. Scene 2.

Meantime Glycerium has given birth to a son, and the mid-wife Lesbia is represented as giving some directions to the servant, Archilis, who is left in charge during her temporary absence. Simo still thinks this to be all part of a trick which is being played upon him, a mistake which is encouraged by Davos, who puzzles Simo by his apparent willingness to forward the marriage of Pamphilus and Philumena.

The metre 481–4 is Bacchiac Tetrameter. See Introduction on Metres.

481. **Archilis**, cf. 228. One MS. reads *oportent*, cf. Adel. 754 *non te haec pudent?*

482. **signa ad salutem** = *signa salutis*, cf. 138, 320 notes.

483. **ista**, sc. Glycerium.

lavet. The active of this verb is sometimes used intransitively, in the sense of the passive, or rather middle; cf. Haut. 618, Liv. 44. 6.

post dĕinde. Notice the tautology, cf. 106 note: here perhaps purposely put into the mouth of an uneducated woman. *Dĕinde* is here scanned as a trisyllable.

484. **dari bibere.** Three constructions are used to express 'to give to drink':—

(1) *Simple inf.*, as here. Cf. Pl. Pers. 5. 2. 40, Cic. Tusc. 1. 26, 65, Liv. 40. 47. 5. This is a Graecism.

(2) *Subjunctive.* Cf. Pl. Stich. 757 *tum vos date bibat tibicini.*

(3) *Quod with subj.* Cf. Pl. Cist. 1. 1. 19 *nimium dabat quod biberem.*

486. per ecastor scitus, by Tmesis for *perscitus ecastor.* Cf. 455. For the intensive use of *per* cf. 265. *perscitus puer,* 'a very fine boy': for similar use of *scitus* cf. Phor. 110, Pl. Merc. 4. 4. 15. Its more common sense is 'witty, clever, sensible,' cf. Pl. Trin. 764. *Ecastor* is commonly used by women, *edepol* by men; cf. 305 note. *Mecastor* is also found, in which case *me* is acc. of *ego*, as in *mehercle*, *medius fidius.*

488. quom, 'since, because,' is sometimes constructed with the indicative in ante-Augustan writers; cf. infra 623, 771, Phorm. 208, Pl. As. 80-1. In this case it is co-ordinate with *quandoquidem*, which is regularly followed by the indicative, and this may have influenced the construction.

489. vel, 'for example.' This meaning probably arose from an ellipse of a former alternative; 'either other instances might be given *or* this'; cf. Hec. 60, Haut. 568.

credat is a potential subj. Cf. 135 note.

abs was a collateral form of *ab* (cf. ἐκ, ἐξ) used before words beginning with *c, q, t*. As early however as Plautus *abs* is rarely found except before *te*. Cicero always wrote *abs te* up to about 55 B.C. Occasional uses of *abs* in later authors, e. g. Livy, are probably intentional archaisms. In *as-pello, as-porto, as-pernor* (for *as-spernor*), the *b* has fallen out. Cf. Pl. Pers. 1. 3. 79, *abs chorago*, Adel. 254 *abs quivis.*

490. coram, used adverbially. No writer before Cicero employs *oram* as a preposition. Cf. 900.

opus facto, also in 715. Cf. 523 *parato opus*, Liv. 8. 13 *maturato opus est*, Cic. Mil. 19. 49 *properato opus.*

puerperae, *dat. commodi.*

492. itan ... itane. Cf. 189 for a similarly emphatic repetition.

tandem, often used in indignant or excited questions. Cf. infra 875, Phor. 231, Pl. Trin. 642, ib. 987.

idoneus, used as antecedent to *quem*, where *is* more commonly appears in classical prose. Cf. 757.

494. saltem accurate, sc. *me falle.*

495. edixin tibi ? = *nonne edixi tibi?* Cf. 17 note, 238 note, 504.

496. interminatus sum, an intensive of *minari*, only found in Plautus and Terence.

497. credon, etc., a sarcastic question implying 'do you suppose that I believe,' etc.?

498. teneo, 'I see.' Cf. 300.

499. **quid credas?** repeats Simo's *credon*, and so is virtually dependent on *rogas* understood. Cf. 191 note.

quasi. Cf. 372.

500. **mihin quisquam**, sc. *renuntiavit?*

tute. The emphatic particle *-te* is only affixed to *tu* and *te*. In *tutemet*, Haut. 374, it is found in conjunction with another emphasising particle—*met*.

501. **qui.** Cf. 6 note.

istaec, feminine of *istic*, a form of *iste* strengthened by demonstrative affix *-ce*, as in *hic, haec, hoc*, and *illic, illaec, illuc*, or *illoc*.

503. **certe enim**, 'most assuredly.' Cf. 91 note.

non etiam = *nondum*. Cf. 116 note.

504. **egon te?** sc. *pernovi*. Cf. 495 for use of *-ne*.

505. **dari verba.** Cf. 211.

falso? 'am I wrong in thinking so?' This word is often given to Davos, but *dari verba falso* seems an absurd phrase, while it has much force in Simo's mouth.

507. **setius**, a comparative form of *secus* [root *sec-* or *seq-* in *sequor*] : *nilo setius* = ' nevertheless.'

508. **ut sis sciens**, for *ut scias*. Cf. 775. This is an early instance of the tendency of Latin, as of other languages, to become 'analytic;' i. e. to express changes of case, tense, mood, voice, etc. by the addition of separate words, e. g. prepositions, auxiliary verbs, etc., instead of by case-endings or verbal terminations, etc. This latter method is called 'synthetic.' Greek is a good example of a 'synthetic' language, English of an 'analytic' language. Instances of this 'analytic' tendency are found in Euripides, and frequently in Hellenistic Greek.

510. **prorsus** [deriv. *pro-versus*], also found in the collateral forms *prorsum* and *prosus*. The comic writers use all these forms, classical authors only *prorsus*. In post-Augustan times an adjective *prorsus-a-um* came into use, and *prorsa* or *prosa oratio*, and later *prosa* as a substantive gained the meaning of 'prose.' Cf. Quin. 1. 8. 2, etc.

512. **qui** = *quibus*. Cf. 6.

513. **postquam** is often used with historic present instead of the ordinary perfect.

514. **ilico**, from *in-loco*, as Gr. αὐτόθεν, ' on the spot,' used here of time, as in 125.

515. **arcessitum ... ut adferret.** Notice the change of construction from the supine to *ut* with subj.

516. This line is a quotation in *oratio recta* of Glycerium's reason for her action.

moventur = *perturbantur*. Cf. 921.

517. **quid ais?** Cf. 137 note.

quom = *quo tempore*. The use of the indicative implies that in Simo's opinion the reporting of the matter to Pamphilus ought to have been simultaneous with its discovery.

518. **capere**, sc. Glycerium.

519. **igitur** is often used in questions like the English 'then,' cf. 598. The sense is, 'Who then did induce him to give her up, if not I?'

521. **id negoti**, i.e. to break up Pamphilus' connection with Glycerium; cf. 2 note.

idem emphasises the opposition of *mihi* and *tu*. 'Do you for your part none the less persevere, as you are doing, in bringing about this match.'

523. **parato opus.** Cf. 490 note.

527. **Chremem.** Cf. 247 note.

528. **gnato**, *dat. commodi*. Cf. Pl. Trin. 611 *ultro venit Philto oratum filio*.

529. **alias**, 'at another time:' rare in this sense in the comic writers; once in Plautus, Curc. 63; twice in Terence, here and Hec. 80.

532. **atque adeo**, 'and indeed:' cf. 162 note. *Adeo* is thus used with conjunctions, especially *si, sive, aut, vel*; cf. 440, 977, Hec. 524, Cic. Att. 1. 17. 9. Cf. Gr. καὶ μήν.

in ipso tempore, 'at the nick of time;' cf. 758 *veni in tempore*, 783 *per tempus advenis*, 974.

eccum. *Ecce* is found in Plautus and Terence combined with various cases of *is, ille,* and *iste*, e. g. *eccam, eccos, eccas, ecca, eccillum* (which is sometimes contracted into *ellum*), *eccistam*. *Eccum* sometimes stands alone, as in 580, 957, sometimes is followed by an accusative, as here. Cf. 855.

Act III. Scene 3.

Chremes enters on his way to Simo's house, in consequence of a report which has reached his ears that his daughter is to be married to Pamphilus on that very day. He is in no good humour, but Simo manages to talk him over, and Chremes agrees to the match on the assurance that Pamphilus has really broken off all connexion with Glycerium, a statement which Davos is summoned to corroborate.

533. **iubeo Chremetem.** The full phrase is found Adel. 460 *salvere Hegionem plurimum iubeo*. For *Chremetem*, see 247 note.

optato, used as an adverb. Cf. 807 *auspicato*.

534. **aliquot** is also used by Cicero as a nominative without a substantive, Pis. 38.

535. viso, ' I come to see.'

id, is explained by the words *tunc an illi insaniant*, and would not be translated by a separate word.

536. paucis. Cf. 29.

quid ... velim et quod ... quaeris. For this change of construction see 273 note, 650.

538. per te deos. Cf. 834. In this sense *per* is often separated from its object.

Chreme, cf. 247 note.

541. quoius is scanned as one syllable.

543. ne ... obsecra. Donatus notes this construction, in place of *ne* with the subjunctive, as a Graecism; a direct translation of μὴ λιτάνευε. Cf. 384, 868.

546. in rem, 'to the advantage;' cf. Pl. Trin. 628, 748, Capt. 398. In the same sense *ex re*, Pl. Ps. 338. *Ob rem* is found = ' with advantage, usefully,' Phorm. 526. In the opposite sense *ab re*, 'to the disadvantage,' Pl. Trin. 238.

556. ante eamus, 'prevent.' Cf. *antevenire*, Pl. Trin. 911.

557. eius, scanned as one syllable; cf. 541.

558. harum, sc. Glycerium, Mysis, Archilis.

559. redducunt. The Ind. probably indicates Simo's conviction that Pamphilus will, otherwise, relent. The spelling is confirmed by Lucretius, who lengthens the first syllable, and appears as a correction in A.

animum aegrotum. Cf. 193.

560. consuetudine. This word is specially used of lovers' relations to each other; cf. 110, 279, 439.

561. liberali, as opposed to a connection with a *peregrina* like Glycerium.

562. dein is used here like Gr. εἶτα.

sese emersurum, 'will extricate himself.' *Emergere* is occasionally used in a transitive sense; cf. Nep. Att. 11. 1 *quibus ex malis ut se emersit*. The perf. part. is used by Cicero, Livy, Ovid, and Tacitus in a middle sense, e.g. Cic. Div. 2. 68, *tibi subito sum visus emersus e flumine*. The verb is found in its ordinary sense, Eun. 555.

563-4. The compressed style of these lines causes some obscurity. After *posse* must be understood *se emergere*, and *posse* must be supplied both before *habere* and *perpeti*. In 564, *illum*, sc. Pamphilus, is the subject, *hanc*, sc. Philumena, is the object. Translate, ' but I do not think that he can extricate himself, nor that he can be always faithful to her (sc. my daughter), nor that I can endure it' (sc. his unfaithfulness).

565. qui = ' how?'

III. 3. 35-4. 4. *NOTES. LINES* 535-582.   99

istuc and istoc, cf. Adel. 981, are used interchangeably as neut. sing. of *istic;* cf. 501 note.

567. nempe ... denique, 'indeed at the worst.'

huc redit, 'comes to this,' i. e. as explained in next line.

569. si corrigitur. Notice the change of mood from *si eveniat.* Simo wishes to represent the former contingency as doubtful, the latter as probable as he can.

571. firmum, 'steady,' one who will not desert his wife.

572. quid istic ? 'well then,' lit. 'what should I do in that case?' a formula of assent after discussion. Cf. Adel. 133, 350, 956, Pl. Trin. 573.

induxti. For other syncopated forms, see 151 note. *Inducere animum* or *in animum*, 'to resolve,' or 'to come to a conclusion,' are both found; cf. infra, 834, 883, Adel. 68, Hec. 603, Pl. Trin. 704.

573. in me claudier, 'should be impeded as far as I am concerned.' Cf. Eun. 164, Cic. de Off. 2. 15. 55.

claudier. Cf. 203 note.

575. sed quid ais ? 'but I say,' introducing a new point which had been forgotten. Cf. 137 note.

578. num censes faceret ? 'Would he do it, do you suppose? *Censes* is parenthetical, not influencing the construction; cf. 313, 314, Adel. 79.

579. tute adeo. Cf. 162 note.

580. atque eccum. Cf. 532 note.

foras, an accusative pl. of the obsolete *fora* used as an adverb meaning 'motion out of doors;' so *foris*, the ablative, means 'rest out of doors.'

video exire, in later Latin would be *video exeuntem;* cf. Pl. Capt. 1, Bacch. 403.

Act III. Scene 4.

Simo takes Davos into his confidence, and informs him of the successful issue of his negotiations with Chremes. Davos has much ado to conceal his consternation, and when left alone bitterly reproaches himself for his folly.

580. Plautus never begins a scene in the middle of a line as Terence here does.

581. advesperascit. About sunset the bride was escorted by a festal procession from her father's house to her new home.

582. dudum, [deriv. *diu-dum*], 'some time ago,' i. e. 196-8. Cf. 948. In 591 and 840 *dudum* refers to the immediate past, 'just now.' In

Pl. Trin. 608 *quam dudum?* = 'how long ago?' Cf. Phorm. 459 *incertior sum multo quam dudum.*

583. **volgus servorum,** 'the common run of slaves.' Cf. Hec. 600 *volgus mulierum.* For the sentiment see Sen. Ep. 47. 3, *eiusdem adrogantiae proverbium iactatur:* '*totidem hostes esse quot servos.*'

584. **amat.** Cf. 185.

facerem. Cf. 282 note.

585. **adeo.** Cf. 162 note.

586. **fidem,** his (sc. Chremes') promise.

587. **non fuerant nuptiae futurae,** 'the marriage was not to have taken place.' Davos, thinking that Simo is merely keeping up his former deception, does not at first believe that the match has been again arranged. Cf. 542-3.

ea gratia. Cf. 433 note.

588. **vide!** 'look at that!'

591. **perimus,** contracted from *periimus,* which some MSS. read. Davos is beginning to fear that after all Simo may be telling him the truth.

dudum. Cf. 582 note.

593. **optume.** Davos cleverly substitutes *optume* as similar in sound to his startled exclamation *occidi!* which Simo half heard.

594. **modo,** 'directly.' This word is used by Plautus and Terence both of the present time, and of the immediate past: cf. Adel. 289, Pl. Ep. 5. 1. 43, Trin. 908, infra 612, 618.

ut adparetur dicam, 'I will give orders that preparation be made.' *Adparetur* is used impersonally, as in Eun. 583 *dum adparatur, virgo in conclavi sedet. Dicam* = *edicam.*

renuntio. The present is used to express the energy and speed of his movements: cf. Eun. 492-3 *quae volo simul inperabo; postea continuo exeo.* Pl. Trin. 1109.

598. **quiescas,** lit. 'rest easy about it.' Cf. Phor. 670 *ego dabo; quiesce,* ib. 713.

mirum ni. Cf. Pl. Trin. 861 *mira sunt ni,* ib. 495 *mirum quin.*

599. **nullus sum,** 'I am undone.' Cf. Phor. 179, ib. 942.

600. **pistrinum.** Cf. 199.

recta via. In this phrase *via* is more usually omitted. Cf. Phor. 859, Adel. 433.

602. **conieci.** Notice the energy of the word: 'I have pitch-forked.' Cf. 620.

erilem filium = *eri filium.* Cf. Pl. Trin. 602.

604. **em,** seems to be used by the comic poets as = *en,* while *hem* expresses astonishment or other strong emotions.

astutias! accusative of exclamation. Davos is speaking with bitter irony.

quod si quiessem, 'whereas had I kept quiet.' For *quod si* see 258 note.

605. **eccum.** Cf. 532 note.

606. **aliquid,** sc. a sword or spear on which he might fall.

ACT III. SCENE 5.

Pamphilus has just heard from Simo that Chremes has consented to his daughter's marriage. He comes on boiling with rage against Davos by whose advice this catastrophe has been brought about, and is only prevented from taking summary vengeance on the slave by the pressing necessity of his own position.

607. **scelus qui.** Cf. 250. The reading of this line is very doubtful. The MSS. read *qui me perdidit,* or *qui me hodie perdidit.* Neither reading will scan. *Hodie* was probably supplied from 620, and *perdidit* would be the natural gloss on the aposiopesis *qui me* . . . On the stage the sense would be completed by a gesture.

atque, 'and yet.' This adversative sense of *atque* is also found in 225, 525, 640, Adel. 40; though to escape the difficulty some editors alter the MSS. reading to *atqui.*

608. **nulli,** for *nullius.* Pronouns forming the gen. and dat. in *-ius* and *-i* are occasionally declined by Terence like a regular adjective in *-us-a-um;* cf. *alterae* dat. fem. infra 983, Phorm. 928, Haut. 271, Eun. 1004 *mihi solae. Nulli consili* is read also Cic. Rosc. 16. § 48.

609. **me commisisse.** Cf. 245.

futtili, [deriv. *fundo,* cf. *futis,* a water-vessel], lit. 'that which cannot contain,' thence worthless.

610. **pretium ob stultitiam** = *pretium stultitiae.* Cf. 138.

612. Cf. 252.

modo. Cf. 594 note.

613. **ducere.** For this use of the present for future inf. see 379, note.

audeam, deliberative subjunctive. Notice the near connexion of meaning between the future simple *negabo* and the present subjunctive *audeam.*

614. **quid me faciam,** 'what I shall do with myself.' *Facere, fieri, esse,* in the sense of 'to do anything with a person,' 'anything to be done with or happen to a person,' are constructed with the ablative or dative without a preposition, or rarely with *de* and the ablative.

Cf. infra 709, Pl. Trin. 405 *quid factumst eo?* Hor. Sat. 1. 1. 63 *quid facias illi?* Cic. Fam. 14. 4. 3 *quid Tulliola mea fiet?* Pl. Trin. 157 *siquid eo fuerit,* Adel. 996 *sed de fratre quid fiet?*

    nec quidem me, sc. *quid faciam scio.*

  615. Cf. 313 note.

  616. **ehodum.** Cf. 29 note. Note hiatus between *sum* and *ehodum.*

  618. **nempe ut modo,** 'as you did just now, I suppose.' Cf. 594 note.

    tibi ego ut credam. Cf. 263 note.

    furcifer [deriv. *furca—fero*]. The Romans used sometimes to punish their slaves by placing on their necks a fork-shaped yoke to the two ends of which their hands were bound. In cases of grave offence the slave so pinioned was scourged, cf. Liv. 1. 26, ib. 2. 36, Cic. Div. 1. 26. 55; in more venial cases the slave was merely led round the neighbourhood as a warning. Cf. Pl. Pers. 5. 2. 71, Hor. Sat. 2. 7. 66. So *furcifer* came to denote a worthless slave.

  619. **restituas,** a potential subjunctive.

    em quo fretus sim! 'see what a fellow I have been relying on!' *Fretus sim* is virtually dependent on the verbal idea contained in *em*; cf. 604.

  620. **coniecisti.** Cf. 602. Cf. Phor. 689 *qui te ad scopulum e tranquillo auferat.*

  621. **an** introduces the second member of a disjunctive sentence (interrogative or otherwise); the first may be suppressed, as here. The sense is, 'Was all this unexpected, or did I not say...' Cf. 386, 399.

    dixti, syncopated form of *dixisti;* cf. 151 note.

  622. **sine ad me redeam.** The imperative of *sino* is commonly followed by the subjunctive without *ut;* cf. 900. The ordinary construction after the indicative of *sino* is accusative and infinitive. Cf. Adel. 794 *reprime iracundiam atque ad te redi.*

    ei mihi. Cf. 73, 263.

  623. **quom non habeo.** Cf. 488 note.

  624. **praecavere mihi me, haud te ulcisci sinit.** This is a case of Zeugma. The sense requires *cogit* or some similar word before *praecavere.*

    te ulcisci, 'to take vengeance on you.'

Act IV. Scene 1.

Charinus enters, almost distracted by what he believes to be the selfish treachery of his friend. Pamphilus with difficulty vindicates his own sincerity, and diverts the wrath of Charinus on to Davos' head, who, though at his wit's end, engages to find some way out of the predicament.

625. The agitation of Charinus is expressed by the metre, line 625 being a dactylic tetrameter, and 626 to 634 Cretic tetrameters.

vecordia. The prefix *ve-* either negatives the positive idea of the simple word, as in *ve-cors, ve-grandis, ve-iovis* (an anti-Jove), or strengthens the simple word, as in *ve-pallidus, ve-stigo*.

ut siet. Cf. 263 note.

627. **gaudeant ... comparent.** The plural verbs are used after the indefinite notion contained in *quoiquam*.

628. **alterīus.** In the Cretic metre a doubtful syllable, which is commonly scanned short, is not unfrequently lengthened when it stands at the end of a foot; e. g. *alterīus, modō* 630, *ubī* 631.

629. **verum,** 'right;' cf. Cic. Leg. 2. 5. 11 *quod est rectum verum quoque est*.

immo, 'yes indeed.' *Immo* more commonly contradicts what precedes, cf. 655, 709, but it is never used as an independent negative like *minime*. In all cases it introduces some important qualification: so, in the present case, the sense is, 'Ah, surely it cannot be true. Yes indeed ...'

630. **modo ... paulum,** 'just a little while before.'

quis, etc., 'who are afraid to say no.'

632. **se aperiunt,** 'they show themselves in their true light.'

633. The line is obscure and doubtful. Translate, 'they are ashamed to refuse the fulfilment of their promise, and yet circumstances press them to do so.' This gives a very unusual sense to *premit*, the reading of all the best MSS. but one; and many editors print *cogit* on the authority of D. It is however scarcely worth while to discuss an uncommon phrase in what is probably only a gloss.

635. **quor meam tibi?** 'why should I give up my bride to you?' an elliptical phrase.

636. **heus,** an interjection commonly used to attract attention, e. g. *heus tu*; sometimes it is a mere emphatic exclamation, as here and Eun. 276.

proximus sum egomet mihi. A proverb like 'Number One comes first.' Cf. Pl. Trin. 1154 *tunica propior palliost*.

638. **verentur,** 'they have scruples.' Notice *illic ... ibi*, a double antecedent to *ubi*. The MSS. read *hic ubi opust non verentur; illic ubi nil opust ibi verentur*. This cannot be scanned, and is plainly a gloss.

639. **agam ... adeam,** deliberative subjunctives.

expostulem? 'should I complain of?' cf. Adel. 595.

640. **multa mala,** i. e. *multa maledicta*.

atque. Cf. 607 note.

641. morem gessero, 'I shall have gratified ;' cf. Adel. 214, 431.

642. respiciunt, sc. *nos;* cf. Phor. 817 *di nos respiciunt.*

643. itane is similarly used in an ironical question, 399.

causa, 'excuse.' Charinus bitterly emphasises '*tandem.*'

644. ducere. Cf. 180.

postulas? 'do you expect?' cf. 331, 657.

645. complacita est, 'she pleased you also.' *Complaceo* is found in no writer of the Augustan age. A perfect active is found Pl. Rud. 727 *Veneri hace complacuerunt;* but the passive form is more common, cf. Haut. 773, Pl. Rud. 187.

646. spectavi, 'I judged.'

647. falsus's = *falleris,* 'you are wrong.'

The MSS. read *nonne;* cf. 238 note.

solidum gaudium, 'genuine joy;' cf. *solidum beneficium,* Eun. 871, infra 964, Pl. Trin. 850, 892.

648. lactasses. This is a frequentative formed from *lacio,* whence *allicio;* cf. *oblecto.* It means ' to cajole.' *Lacto* is also used 912, and in Pl. Cist. 2. 1. 9.

649. habeas. Cf. 889.

habeam. Cf. 191, 282, Pl. Trin. 133.

650. hic, δεικτικῶς, i. e. pointing to Davos.

confecit; rather an uncommon use of the word, but cf. Haut. 1003. We should have expected a subjunctive corresponding to *vorser.* For a similar change cf. 273, 536, Pl. Most. 199. Donatus mentions another reading, *conflavit.*

651. de te. *Ex* is used instead of *de,* Adel. 416 *ex aliis sumere exemplum sibi.*

653. altercasti, ἅπαξ λεγόμενον in the active in classical Latin: *altercatur* is found as an impersonal passive in Justinian, but the classical usage is *altercari* as a deponent.

dudum, sc. in Act ii. Sc. 5; cf. 582 note. Charinus is of course speaking ironically.

655. immo etiam, 'no indeed;' cf. 629 note, 673, 708.

quo tu minus... meas. The sense is, 'And from what you say (*quo = et eo*) you are quite ignorant of any troubles.'

656. haec. Cf. 328 note.

657. postulabat. Cf. 331, 644.

nunc, of course goes with *dare.*

660. enicas, [deriv. a Sanskrit root meaning 'to disappear,' whence Lat. *neco, nex,* Gr. νέκυς, νεκρός]. *Enico* seems to be more correct than *eneco.*

661. The order is, '*ut dicerem patri (me) esse ducturum*, sc. *uxorem*. Some of the good MSS. insert *me* before *esse*, but it spoils the metre.

662. suadere, orare, may be constructed after *destitit*, or may be taken as historical infinitives.

usque adeo ... Cf. Pl. Cist. 2. 3. 40 *instare usque adeo donec se adiurat anus*.

663. quis homo istuc, sc. *fecit?* For *istuc*, cf. 565 note.

The readings of lines 663-4 are uncertain. The text follows the best MSS.

interturbat, 'he turns everything upside down;' a rare word; cf. Pl. Bacch. 733 *ne interturba*.

664. qui auscultaverim, 'because I listened to him.'

665. scelus. Cf. 607.

Notice the hiatus between *factum* and *hem*. It is sufficiently accounted for by the change of speakers; see Introduction on Metres.

666. at is often used in curses and passionate exclamations; cf. Eun. 431, Hec. 134, Pl. Most. 655, Verg. A. 2. 535. It is rarely used in blessing or entreaty; cf. Pl. Pers. 4. 3. 18, Verg. A. 8. 572.

duint, archaic for *dent*, as *perduint* for *perdant;* cf. Phor. 519, 976, 1005. Terence also uses *duim, duit*, Hec. 134, Phor. 713. Plautus employs all the following, *duim, duis* or *duas, duit, duint*.

667. coniectum. Cf. 602, 620.

670. successit, used impersonally.

671. processit=*successit*, cf. 679, Adel. 897. Notice the alliteration.

673. immo etiam. Cf. 629 note, 655, 709.

satis credo is parenthetical; cf. 313 note.

675. pro servitio, lit. 'conformably to my position as slave,' i.e. 'as a slave.' For a similar sense of *pro* cf. Phor. 195 *satis pro imperio*, Adel. 427 *pro mea sapientia*, and often in Cicero, Livy, etc.

676. manibus pedibus. Cf. 161. Notice the asyndeton, cf. 680, i.e. omission of a conjunction, followed by the polysyndeton, i.e. redundance of conjunctions in *noctesque et dies*. This gives great emphasis to the sentence. Cf. Adel. 64.

677. dum, 'if only.' Sometimes *dum* is thus used without a verb following, e.g. Phor. 526 *minume dum ob rem*.

680. vel, used as an intensive particle with the imperative; cf. Phor. 143.

missum face. For the phrase cf. infra 833, Eun. 90. *Face=fac* is frequent in Plautus and Terence, e.g. infra 712, 821, 833, Pl. Trin. 800, etc. Notice the blunt turn given to the sentence by the asyndeton.

681. The sense is, 'I want to devise something better for myself: do you restore me to the position wherein you found me.'

682. concrepuit ostium. Greek doors opened outwards, and so it was customary on leaving a house to knock against the door as a warning to persons in the street. The door was said *crepare, concrepare,* Gr. ψοφεῖν; cf. Phor. 840. The visitor was said *pellere,* κόπτειν, κρούειν, Adel. 638, 788; or, if violent, *pulsare, pultare,* ἀράσσειν, Adel. 633, 637. Davos is naturally delighted at this interruption, which gives him a little more time, while Pamphilus impatiently tries to keep him to the point.

683. nil ad te, sc. *attinet.*

quaero, 'I am thinking;' cf. 702.

nuncine = *num-ce-ne;* cf. *sicine,* 689. The sense is, 'are you now at last beginning to think?'

inventum dabo. Cf. 684, 703. Greek writers have a similar use of a participle with τίθημι; e.g. Aesch. Ag. 32 τὰ δεσποτῶν γὰρ εὖ πεσόντα θήσομαι.

Act IV. Scene 2.

Mysis is reassured by Pamphilus, who swears eternal fidelity to Glycerium. Davos devises a new plot.

684. ubi ubi = *ubicumque,* is very rare: cf. Enn. 1042.

inventum curabo et adductum. Cf. 683.

688. integrascit, is ἅπαξ λεγόμενον.

689. sicine. Cf. 683 note. For accusative and infinitive in indignant questions, see 245 note.

tua, is spoken to Davos.

691. quibus, sc. *nuptiis.*

potuerat quiesci, used impersonally; *quiesci* being followed by the ablative. 'And how easily could this have been kept quiet, if he had kept quiet.' Note the combined alliteration and assonance.

hic, pointing to Davos, δεικτικῶς, as so often in Comedy.

693. Mysis refers to the last words of Pamphilus, 690.

694. adiuro is followed here and Hec. 268-9 by accusative and infinitive, in Pl. Bacch. 777, by *ut* and subjunctive: the former construction is usual in later Latin.

696. contigit, sc. *haec,* 'she became mine.'

valeant, 'away with those who..;' cf. Adel. 622: χαίρειν is similarly used.

698. **resipisco,** 'I recover myself, breathe again.' In Haut. 843-4 *te intellego resipisse* means, 'I see that you have come to your senses again.'

non Apollinis, etc. Other instances of the Delphic oracle alluded to as the standard of certainty are found in Pl. Pseud. 480, Lucr. I. 736, Cic. Ep. ad Brut. I. I. 6.

atque for *quam* after comparatives is sometimes found in negative sentences, e. g. Pl. Merc. 897, Cas. 5. I. 7; later poets, especially Horace, use *atque* thus, even in affirmative sentences : e. g. Hor. Epod. 15. 5.

699. **ut ne** = *ut non*, to signify a negative result, e. g. Pl. Trin. 105. Cf. Hec. 595, Eun. 942. Cicero occasionally, Livy twice, Caesar never uses *ut ne* = *ne:* Horace has *quo ne,* Sat. 2. I. 37. For *qui ne* = *ut ne* see 335; for *ut ne* = *ne* see 258.

701. **in proclivi,** 'easy:' cf. Pl. Capt. 336 *tam hoc quidem tibi in proclivist, quam imber est, quando pluit.*

702. **quis videor?** 'What do you think of me?' Pamphilus is expecting some applause for his heroic resolve, an expectation somewhat damped by his friend's depressing reply.

Notice that the final syllable of *ego,* as of *tibi* 703, and *cedo* 705, is considered as long when standing at the end of the fourth foot in a septenarius. See Introduction on Metres.

703. Pamphilus lays sneering emphasis on *conere;* hence Davos' rejoinder.

effectum reddam. Cf. 683 note.

704. **quin,** a corroborative particle, 'yes, indeed:' cf. 45 note.

ne erres. Davos wishes to be clearly understood that his plan is merely to frustrate the match proposed by Simo for Pamphilus, not to procure the bride for Charinus.

707. **vos amolimini,** 'pack yourselves off:' *amoliri* is not found elsewhere in Terence, though Plautus uses it six times.

708. **ego hanc visam.** Notice the scansion: see Introduction on Metres.

quo hinc te agis? 'where are you going to?' *se agere,* 'to betake oneself,' 'to come,' 'to go,' is a common phrase in Plautus, e. g. Trin. 1078. Terence uses it here only, Vergil in A. 6. 337, 8. 465, 9. 696.

709. **quid me fiet?** Cf. 614 note.

710. **dieculam,** a diminutive of *dies,* found here only in Terence, and but once in Plautus : used by Cicero.

711. **quantum** = ὅσον.

promoveo, 'I put off,' not elsewhere found in this sense in any author. Terence uses *promoveo* in only three other places, and always as 'to accomplish :' cf. supra 640, Eun. 913, Hec. 703.

quid ergo? 'what do you say?' *Ergo* is used thus in Plautus and Terence to make a question more emphatic : cf. Pl. Trin. 988, *Ch. Ipsus, inquam, Charmides sum? Sy. Ergo ipsusne es?* ib. 901: infra 850 *tibi ergo*.

712. ut ducam. Supply *id age* or some similar phrase.

face. Cf. 680 note.

siquid poteris, sc. *pro me efficere*.

713. age, 'all right.' Compare the Old English 'go to.'

714. dum exeo. Cf. 329 note.

715. factost opus. Cf. 490 note.

Act IV. Scene 3.

Mysis left alone is startled by the appearance of Davos with Glycerium's baby. Davos bids her lay the infant at Simo's door, when the unexpected approach of Chremes introduces a new complication.

716. nilne esse... Cf. 245 note.

proprium = Gr. βέβαιον, cf. Menander, Monost. 655 βέβαιον οὐδὲν ἐν βίῳ δοκεῖ πέλειν : infra 960, Vergil E. 7. 31 *si proprium hoc fuerit*, where see Conington's note, Cic. Man. 16, &c.

di, vostram fidem, 'heaven help us.' The full phrase, *di, obsecro vostram fidem*, 'Ye gods, I implore your aid,' is found Pl. Amph. 1130 and elsewhere. *Fides* means originally 'confidence ;' then that which produces confidence, ' truth, promise ;' then a promise given to a suppliant, i. e. 'aid,' 'protection :' cf. 237 note, 246.

718. amicum... Notice the climax. Cf. 295.

loco, ' vicissitude.'

720. facile. We have a similar use of ' easily ' in colloquial language. Notice that *facile* is regularly used as an adverb: *faciliter* is not classical.

laborem, 'distress,' cf. 831 ; so used by Vergil.

hic... illic, 'now... then.'

723. exprompta malitia, ' ready craft :' so Pl. Ep. 4. 1. 19 *muliebris adhibenda malitia nunc est*. Several MSS. read *memoria* for *malitia*.

724. ocius, ' with all speed.' This comparative is not unfrequently so used : e. g. infra 731, Phor. 562.

726. humine. Mysis naturally hesitates to lay a new-born infant on the cold stones of the street.

ex ara. Two altars used to stand at the front of the Roman stage, one on the right sacred to Dionysus in tragedy and Apollo in comedy, one on the left to the god or goddess in whose honour the festival was celebrated; in this case to Magna Mater or Cybele. See note on the title. An altar also stood at the entrance of every Roman house.

verbenas, the boughs of the sacred trees, such as laurel, olive, myrtle, with which altars were wreathed. Such boughs were borne by *Fetiales* and suppliant priests: they were also used in sacrificial and other rites. Cf. Verg. E. 8. 65, ib. A. 12. 120, and Conington's notes on these passages. Donatus gives the derivation '*verbenae quasi herbenae.*' Servius on Verg. E. 8. 65 gives '*a viriditate.*'

728. **ad erum iurandum mihi**. The MSS. have *iusiurandum*, against the metre, a reading rejected by all editors from Donatus downwards. It seems on the whole best to consider *iurandum* to be for *iurandum esse*, an impersonal gerundive constructed after *opus sit;* and to take *ad herum* as = *apud herum*; cf. Pl. Cist. 1. 1. 100 *iuravit apud matrem meam.* Translate, 'if by chance it may be necessary for me to take an oath before my master.' R. Klotz thinks that *iurandum* is put for *iurare* by a sort of attraction. Others consider that *iurandum* here = *iusiurandum*, quoting Pl. Cist. 2. 1. 26, but the reading in that passage is very doubtful, and such an ellipse would be against all analogy, though the construction would in that case find a parallel in 740. Bentley and others evade the difficulty by reading *iurato*.

729. **liquido**, is one of a fairly numerous class of ablatives used as adverbs, e.g. *continuo, crebro, serio*, etc. Cf. 533.

730. **religio**, 'scruple.'
    istaec. Cf. 501 note.

731. **ocius**. Cf. 724. Construe *porro* with *agam*.

732. **pro Iuppiter**. Cf. 237 note.

733. **consilium**. Davos had probably intended to tell Simo that the baby had been laid at his door.

735-6. 'See that you support my story with a word or two, whenever necessary.'

738. **quod mea opera opus sit vobis**, 'wherein my aid may be needed by you:' *quod* is an acc. of respect; cf. 289. For *opus* with a personal construction, see 740.

aut is the MSS. reading which most editors have altered to *ut*, needlessly. The sense is, 'if there is anything which I can do, or if you see any further reason (i.e. to make my presence desirable), I will remain.'

ACT IV. SCENE 4.

An amusing scene follows. Davos, pretending to know nothing about the matter, bullies Mysis into saying before Chremes that the baby belongs to Pamphilus, while giving her contradictory orders apart, till the poor old woman becomes almost distracted. Chremes at once resolves to break off the match.

740. **quae opus fuere ad nuptias.** Cf. 728, 738 notes.

744. **di vostram fidem.** Cf. 237, 716 note.

745. **illi**, archaic for *illic*, found in Plautus, Terence, and perhaps Vergil G. 1. 54, 1. 251, 3. 17: here required by the metre.

quid hominum litigant, 'what a lot of people have cases on.' Cf. Pl. Poen. 3. 3. 5, *sed quid hic tantum hominum incedunt?* A similar *constructio* κατὰ σύνεσιν is often found after *pars, quisque, uterque*, etc., e. g. Pl. Trin. 35 *faciunt pars hominum*.

746. **annona carast**, 'prices are high.' *Annona*, from *annus*, means (1) the yearly produce; (2) food, especially corn; (3) the price of grain or other food; (4) the market. Cf. Pl. Trin. 484 *cena hac annona est sine sacris hereditas*.

747. **quae haec est fabula?** 'what farce is this?' For *fabula*, 'a comedy,' see Prologue 3 and 16; 'a story,' 925; *fabulae*, 'stuff and nonsense,' 224.

749. **rogites.** Subjunctive with causal relative.

752-3. **verbum si ... faxis.** Cf. 178, 860. For *faxis* cf. 854 note.

754. **male dicis?** 'do you abuse me?' referring to *deliras*.

dic clare, 'speak up;' i. e. so that Chremes may hear.

757. **adeon videmur**, etc. Cf. 492. For *adeo* cf. 162 note.

758. **in quibus inludatis**, a construction not found elsewhere. Terence uses *inludere* in three other places with the direct accusative, infra 822, Phorm. 915 *satis superbe inluditis me*, Haut. 741; once with *in* and acc., Eun. 942. Cicero uses both these constructions and also the dative, which latter construction is also found in Vergil and Tacitus. Its usual meaning is 'to make game of,' so 'to stake,' as in 822; very rarely 'to sport with,' as in Hor. Sat. I. 4. 139.

in tempore. Cf. 532.

759. **adeo** has an intensive force, 'make all haste.' Cf. 162 note.

760. **excessis** = *excesseris*. Notice *manē, cavē*. Cf. Introduction on Metres.

761. **di te eradicent**, more emphatic than *di te perdant*. The same phrase is found Haut. 589; and *eradicare* is used several times by Plautus, but by no other classical author.

762. **at**, expressing indignation. Cf. 666 note.

763. **quoium.** This interrogative pronoun is not uncommon in the comic writers, e. g. infra 932, Pl. Trin. 45 *quoia hic vox prope me sonat?*

but is rare elsewhere, though found Verg. E. 3. 1 *dic mihi, Damoeta, cuium pecus?* ib. E. 5. 87.

765. **vostri,** sc. *eri.*

768. **quemne,** 'what? the one which?' Cf. Phor. 923 *argentum rursum iube rescribi, Phormio. Ph. quodne ego discripsi porro* . . .

769. **O hominem audacem.** Notice the hiatus after *O.* Cf. infra 817, Adel. 183, 304.

770. **suffarcinatam,** 'with a bundle under her cloak.'

771. **aliquot adfuerunt liberae.** The evidence of slaves was not received at Athens except under torture, and at Rome no slave could give evidence against his master except in special cases. Cf. Phor. 292–3 *servom hominem causam orare leges non sinunt, neque testimoni dictiost.* For the indicative after *quom,* 'because.' cf. supra 488 note, 623.

772. **ne.** Cf. 324 note.

775. **nunc adeo.** Cf. 162 note.

ut sis sciens. Cf. 508 note.

777. **provolvam teque pervolvam,** 'I will tumble him over, and roll you along.'

778–9. **fallacia,** etc. . . . 'one trick treads on the heels of another.'

780. See 220 sqq.

781. **eam** is contracted into one syllable and then cut off. See Introduction on Metres.

782. **iocularium in malum,** 'into a ludicrous scrape.' Cf. Phor. 134 *iocularem audaciam. Iocularium* is ἅπαξ λεγόμενον.

783. **per tempus** = *in tempore,* 532, 758.

787. **hic,** δεικτικῶς, pointing to Chremes.

non in poetry and late prose is occasionally used for *ne,* although Quintilian 1. 5. 50 mentions it as a solecism. Cf. Verg. A. 12. 78 *non Teucros agat in Rutulos;* Hor. S. 2. 5. 91 *non etiam sileas.* In like manner *neque* is sometimes used for *neve* even by Cicero and Quintilian, who, in spite of his condemnation of *non feceris* 1. 5. 50, himself writes *non desperemus* 7. 1. 56, and *non assuescat* 2. 16. 6. Cf. Mad. § 456. obs. 2, and § 459. In the present case the fact that the negation really belongs to *Davom* may have suggested the use of *non.*

789. **ne me attigas.** *Attigere,* the older form of *attingere,* is not found in any later author than Terence. Plautus uses it several times, but in all certain cases in 2nd pers. of pres. subj. in prohibitions.

790. Mysis was going to finish her sentence with some such words as *narrabo, peream.*

792. **socer,** i.e. *sponsae pater.* Cf. 732. A similar proleptic use of *gener* and *adfinis* may be found in Pl. Trin. 422, 622, Verg. A. 2. 344.

793. **praediceres,** 'you should have told me before.' This is really an apodosis, a protasis such as *si recte faceres* being suppressed. Cf. 138. Such a use of the imperf. for the pluperf. is an idiom often found in the best authors; sometimes even the pres. subj. is substituted for an imperf. or pluperf. Cf. Mad. § 347. obs. 1, 2, 3.

794–5. Translate, 'do you suppose it makes little difference whether all your acts are sincere and natural, or all premeditated?'

Davos means that Mysis would certainly have betrayed herself had she attempted to act a part; the only chance was to keep her in the dark, so that she could speak and act naturally.

796. **platea,** 'a street.' Gr. ἡ πλατεῖα ὁδός. In spite of the derivation the scansion is *platĕa*. Cf. Pl. Trin. 840, Hor. Ep. 2. 2. 71 *purae sunt plateae*, Cat. 15. 7.

799. **lege.** By a law of Solon the property of a person dying intestate passed to the nearest of kin. Cf. Aristoph. Av. 1660 sqq. Property was said *lege redire ad aliquem, testamento venire*. Cf. Hec. 171–2.

800. **obsecro,** 'heaven help us.' Cf. Eun. 963.

801. **sobrinus,** contracted from *sororinus*, properly a mother's sister's child, i. e. a first cousin on the mother's side.

803. **itan Chrysis—?** 'is Chrysis really—?' Crito avoids the ill-omened word 'dead' by a discreet *aposiopesis*, and a slight cough.

nos ... miseras perdidit, 'she has left us poor souls disconsolate.'

804. The verbs to be supplied are, '*quid vos agitis? quo pacto hic vivitis? satine recte valetis?*

sic, 'so so.' Cf. Phor. 145 *quid rei gerit? G. sic, tenuiter.*

805. This proverb is found among the fragments of Menander, ζῶμεν γὰρ οὐχ ὡς θέλομεν ἀλλ' ὡς δυνάμεθα, and still earlier in Plato, Hipp. Mai. 301. Caecilius used it before Terence in a Latin dress, '*vivas ut possis, quando non quis ut velis*,' and Plautus alludes to it Pers. 1. 1. 17. Latin writers introduce a proverb by *aiunt*. Cf. Phor. 506, 768.

ACT IV. SCENE 5.

At this point appears Crito, a relation of Chrysis, and her heir-at-law. He is much perturbed at hearing that Glycerium has not discovered her parents.

807. **utinam,** 'would that she had.' Cicero is rather fond of using *utinam* elliptically, especially after *quod*.

an is often found in a question apparently simple, but which must be regarded as the second member of an alternative question, the former being inferred from the context. *An nondum etiam?* is here the second member of *iam hic suos parentis repperit?*

auspicato. Cf. 533, 729 notes.

adpuli, the reading of all the best MSS., has been altered on very slender authority to *attuli* by Fleckeisen. Crito had come by sea, and *navem adpellere* was a common phrase.

808. tetulissem. Cf. 832 *tetulit*. These reduplicated tenses of *fero* are not found elsewhere in Terence, but are not uncommon in Plautus : *tetulerunt* is once used by Lucretius, 6. 672. These forms are from a root *tol-*, or *tul-*, found in τλῆναι, τάλας, tollo, tolerare, (t)latus.

811. lites sequi. Gr. δίκην διώκειν. Cf. Adel. 248, Phor. 408.

quam . . . utile. This is, of course, ironical.

814. grandiuscula, ἅπαξ λεγόμενον, 'pretty well grown up.' This is read by all MSS., but some editors alter it to *grandicula* to avoid the synizesis. Cf. Haut. 515 *tardiusculus*.

clamitent, 'people would cry out.' a potential subjunctive. This use of the indefinite plural is not usual ; an impersonal construction is far more common.

815. sycophantam. By Athenian law successful prosecutors of public offenders received rewards, often half the penalty, political jealousy always gave support to an accusation, and wealthy citizens were often ready to avert vexatious proceedings by a substantial payment.

All this encouraged the growth of an unscrupulous class of men who made their livelihood by laying informations, extorting money under threats of so doing, and similar disreputable practices.

These men were called συκοφάνται. Their name was derived from σῦκος, a fig, and φαίνειν, to lay information, because an ancient law against the exportation of figs, though unrepealed, became practically obsolete, and consequently prosecutions under it were considered peculiarly vexatious. By an easy transition, a sycophant came to mean a swindler or pettifogger of any description. See infra 919, Pl. Trin. iv. sc. 2, Aristoph. Achar. 818, Aves 1410, Plut. 850.

816. non lubet, i.e. Crito's own good feeling would prevent him.

817. Notice the hiatus in *O optume*, as in 769.

antiquom obtines, 'you keep old-fashioned honesty'; an elliptical phrase. Cf. Hec. 860 *ac tu ecastor morem antiquom atque ingenium obtines*. For similar uses of *antiquos* cf. Adel. 442, Pl. Trin. 72, 381, Most. 989, etc.

819. nolo me videat senex, 'I don't want the old man (sc. Simo) to see me.' *Nolo* with this construction is very rare, though *volo* followed by the subj. is common enough.

Act V. Scene 1.

Simo in vain tries to persuade Chremes that the story about Glycerium and her baby is only part of a plot to break off the match.

820. **spectata**, ' proved.'
821. **incepi adire**, 'I was on the brink.'
    face. Cf. 680 note, 833.
822. **inlusi vitam filiae**, 'staked my daughter's life.' Cf. 758 note.
823. **immo enim**, ' nay indeed.' *Enim* is here intensive ; cf. 91 note.
824. **dudum**, 'a little while ago' ; cf. 582 note.
825. **prae studio**, 'from your eagerness.'
826. **cogitas**, etc., 'you consider neither the bounds of my compliance, nor the bearing of your request.' For the mixed construction see 49–50.
827. **remittas**, ' you would cease'; cf. 904 *mitte orare*.
828. **at.** Cf. 666 note.
829. **re uxoria.** A common periphrasis ; cf. *res divina, res rustica, res frumentaria*, etc.
830. **seditionem.** Cf. Cic. Att. 2. 1. 5 *ea est enim seditiosa, ea cum viro bellum gerit.*
    incertas, because a divorce might be feared at any moment.
831. **eius.** Notice the emphatic repetition. It is scanned as one syllable.
    labore. Cf. 720 note.
832. **tetulit.** For the meaning cf. 188, for the form cf. 808 notes.
    feras, ' be content,' lit. ' bear with it.'
833. **hinc civem**, i.e. an Athenian citizen ; cf. 908.
    missos face. Cf. 680 note, 821.
834. **per ego te deos oro.** For the separation of *per* from its case cf. supra 538, Verg. A. 4. 314, 12. 56, Liv. 23. 9. 2, etc.
    ut ne. Cf. 259 note.
    illis. sc. Glycerium and her attendants.
    credere. The subj. with *ut* or *ne* is used after *animum inducere*, as well as the inf., both by the comedians and by Cicero.
835. **illum**, sc. Pamphilus.
836. **nuptiarum gratia**, 'on account of the marriage,' i.e. to break it off.
838. **ea causa quam ob rem.** Cf. 382.
840. **facturas**, sc. Glycerium and her servants.
    dudum praedixit. Cf. 507, 582 note.

841. nescio qui, 'somehow or other.' The MSS. reading *nescio quid* is almost certainly due to an ignorant correction; such lines as 340, Adel. 79, give no support to the use of *nescio quid* in the above sense. The logical order is, '*et volui dicere tibi, ac nescio qui sum oblitus.*' For the ὕστερον πρότερον, as Grammarians term such an inversion, cf. Verg. A. 2. 353 *moriamur et in media arma ruamus.*

Act V. Scene 2.

Davos, unaware of the presence of Simo and Chremes, comes out of Glycerium's house. In his confusion he mentions that Pamphilus is now with her, and to shield himself tells Chremes of Crito's assertion that Glycerium is an Athenian citizen. Simo, in a fury, shouts for Dromo, the slave who flogged for the household, by whom Davos is carried off bodily for summary punishment. Simo summons Pamphilus from the house.

842. nunciam. Cf. 171 note.

    em Davom tibi, 'see you Davos there'; *tibi* is Ethic dative. Cf. Eun. 472 *em Eunuchum tibi,* Pl. Trin. 185 *em meam avaritiam tibi.* For *em* cf. 604 note.

843. hospitis, sc. Crito.

845. in vado. Cf. 480, *ego in portu navigo.*

848. arcesse, 'send for them,' sc. the bridal party; cf. 581.

    bene sane, 'mighty fine.'

    id enim, etc., 'that certainly is all that's wanted now'; *enim* is intensive, cf. 91, 206 notes.

    hinc, lit. 'from present circumstances;' cf. Pl. Epid. 1. 1. 25 *at unum a praetura tua abest.*

849. etiam tu hoc responde. This reading is kept in deference to the MSS. and Servius. Many editors adopt the reading of Donatus *respondes,* because *etiam* is so often used with impatient questions, e.g. Adel. 550 *etiam taces?* Phor. 542 *etiam tu hinc abis?* etc. The imperative is however found with *etiam,* Hec. 841, Pl. Most. 2. 2. 43, etc.

    istic, δεικτικῶς, pointing to Glycerium's house.

    est. For the indicative cf. 45 note.

    ita, 'yes.' An affirmative answer may also be expressed by *etiam, vero, verum, sane, factum;* or by repeating the verb, e.g. *hoc facies? faciam;* or by a pronoun, e.g. *hoc facies? ego vero.*

850. tibi ergo, 'yes you': *ergo* is more commonly used as an emphatic particle in questions, cf. 711 note.

    quam dudum. Cf. 582 note.

852. dixti. Cf. 151 note.

853. quid illum censes? 'what do you think he would be doing?' This phrase probably originated in an ellipse of *facere*; cf. Adel. 656 *quid ipsae? quid aiunt?* Mi. *quid illas censes?* Pl. Triu. 811 *quid illum putas?* For illustration of this sarcasm see 552.

854. immo vero. Davos replies to Chremes' sneer by representing Pamphilus as present in Glycerium's house to interview Crito, whom Davos pretends to think an impostor.

faxo=*fecero*. A future perfect is often used in Plautus and Terence to express a quickly completed future action, where in English we should employ the future simple. *Faxo* in Terence is found four times with the fut. ind., cf. Phor. 308 *iam faxo hic aderit*, ib. 1055, Eun. 285, 663, twice with the pres. subj., cf. Adel. 209 *cupide accipiat faxo*, ib. 847 *coquendo sit faxo*, following the subj. in both cases. Here the MSS. read *audias*, but several editors have altered it to *audies*. There is no certain instance of the fut. after *faxo* in Plautus, and the Augustan writers invariably use the subjunctive construction.

855. ellum. Cf. 532 note, Pl. Trin. 622.

confidens, 'audacious'; commonly used, as here, in a bad sense. Cf. Phor. 122–3 *est parasitus quidam Phormio, homo confidens*.

catus, 'shrewd,' like *confidens*, can be used in both a good and a bad sense.

857. tristis veritas, 'a stern honesty.'

860. Spengel scans this line as trochaic, beginning *Drŏmŏ Drŏmŏ*, cf. 760. In Roman households the slave whose special duty it was to flog others was called *lorarius*.

861. sublimem hunc intro rape, 'up with him and carry him in.' Cf. Adel. 316 *sublimem medium arriperem*, Pl. Mil. Gl. 1394. In these and other passages some editors read *sublimen*, an adverb, against the MSS.

quantum potest. Cf. 327 note. The impersonal use of *potest* in this and similar phrases is so general that we have admitted it here on the authority of Donatus.

864. commotum reddam, 'I will have you touched up.' Cf. 683 note.

tamen etsi = *tametsi* in later Latin.

865. quadrupedem constringito, 'bind him hand and foot.' At Athens a refractory slave sometimes had his neck thrust into a wooden collar, κύφων, and his hands and feet tied together like a calf.

868. et illi, sc. *Pamphilo ostendam quid sit pericli fallere patrem.*

ne saevi. Cf. 543 note.

869. pietatem gnati! 'my undutiful son.' Acc. of exclamation. Cf. 876, 948, 956.

870. For the infinitive cf. 245 note.

Act V. Scene 3.

Simo bitterly upbraids his son, accusing him, moreover, of having suborned Crito. Pamphilus begs to be allowed to clear himself by fetching Crito.

872. **quis me volt.** Cf. 29 note.
874. **gravius,** 'too hard.'
   possiet. Cf. 234 note.
876. **O ingentem confidentiam,** 'O monstrous impudence!' Cf. 855, 869 notes.
879. **adeo inpotenti esse animo,** 'to be of a disposition so uncontrollable.' Notice, however, that *adeo* qualifies the whole sentence, not *inpotenti* alone, as if it were *tam*. For *esse* cf. 245 note. In Pl. Trin. 131 we find *adulescenti animi inpoti*, where *animi* is gen. depending on *inpoti*.
882. **me miserum!** 'wretch that I am!'
   id, sc. your wretchedness.
   sensti. Cf. 151 note.
883. **olim istuc,** sc. *sentire debuisti.*
   animum induxti tuom. Cf. 151, 572 notes.
887. **huius.** Simo is so deeply wounded by his son's undutiful conduct that he turns from him in bitter disgust, and speaks of him contemptuously as 'this fellow.' Scan *huius* as a monosyllable.
890. **huius,** sc. *mei.* Cf. 310 note.
892. **viceris,** 'have your own way.' The future perfect is sometimes used as a virtual imperative. Cf. Adel. 437 *ille ad me attinet, quando ita volt frater; de istoc ipse viderit;* Liv. 1. 58 *vos, inquit, videritis quid illi debeatur;* Verg. A. 10. 743 *nunc morere; ast de me divom pater atque hominum rex Viderit.* In this case *viceris* implies indignant concession; *viderit* or *viderint* similarly imply the abandonment of the question in point.
893. **licetne pauca,** sc. *dicere.*
894. **tamen,** i.e. notwithstanding his unfilial conduct, yet hear him.
895. **tandem** seems here to be used in the sense of 'pray,' which is so common in interrogations. It might however be taken in the ordinary way, 'at length,' i.e. after all your invective.
896. Notice the change of metre to trochaic tetrameters.
899. **adlegatum,** 'suborned,' not elsewhere used by Terence. Cf. Pl. Trin. 1142 *meo adlegatu venit.* *Adlegare* = to despatch on a private commission, *legare* on public business.
900. **adducas?** Cf. 191 note.

902. **ne**, regular after *dum*, 'provided that.'
903. **pro peccato magno**, 'to expiate a grave fault.'

Act V. Scene 4.

Chremes recognises Crito as an old acquaintance. Simo abuses him roundly as an impostor. But when Crito tells his tale it is found that Glycerium is really a daughter of Chremes, by name Pasiphila, who with her uncle Phania had been shipwrecked on the island of Andros when sailing to Asia in quest of Chremes many years back. This brings about a happy *dénoûment*. All parties are reconciled. Pamphilus receives a handsome dowry with his Pasiphila, and even Davos is forgiven.

904. **mitte orare.** Cf. 827 *remittas ... onerare.*
    ut faciam, sc. as you desire.
905. **ipsi Glycerio**, *dat. commodi* after *cupio*, as after *consulo*.
906. Chremes and Crito had been acquainted in former days.
907. **quid tu Athenas**, sc. *venisti*.
    evenit, 'accident.' Crito does not choose to tell the real reason at once.
908. **hinc civem.** Cf. 833.
909. **itane huc paratus.** Cf. Phor. 427 *itane es paratus facere me advorsum omnia?*
910. **tune ... haec facias?** 'are you to do this?'
911. **eductos.** Cf. 274 note.
912. **lactas.** Cf. 648 note.
914. **substet**, 'hold his own;' ἅπαξ λεγόμενον in this sense.
    noris ... arbitrere. We should have expected the imperfect subjunctive. Cf. 310, 793 note; Mad. § 347, obs. 1.
915. **hic vir sit bonus?** 'he an honourable man?' *Sit* is in the subjunctive, because the words are in a quotation. Cf. 191 note.
916. **itane.** Cf. 492.
    adtemperate, 'opportunely,' ἅπαξ λεγόμενον.
918. **habeo.** The pres. indic. standing as apodosis of *ni metuam* expresses the *fact* that Pamphilus has some advice to give and would give it but for his fear of Simo.
919. **sycophanta.** Cf. 815 note.
    sic est hic, 'that is his way,' i.e. to use strong language and fly into a passion. Cf. Phor. 527 *sic sum; si placeo, utere.*
    mitte, 'don't mind him.'
    videat qui siet, 'let him see to his way.' For *siet*, cf. 234 note.
921. 'Do I meddle with or care about your concerns?'
922. **dico ... audierim.** This is the reading of A, and means, 'For

now it can be known whether I have heard truly or falsely what I say.' The other MSS. read *dixi . . . audieris,* 'whether you have heard truly or falsely what I said.' Cf. 908.

924. **adplicat . . . se,** i.e. as a client to a patron. Cf. 193, 997 for the same phrase.

et istaec una parva virgo, 'and with him that very woman, then a little girl.'

925. **fabulam inceptat,** 'a pretty tale he is beginning.' Cf. 747 note.

926. **tum** = Gr. εἶτα, 'moreover.'

928. **nomen tam cito tibi?** sc. *dicam.* Crito does not at the moment remember the name.

930. **Rhamnusium.** Rhamnus was an Attic deme lying on the eastern coast, about five miles from Marathon. It contained a fortress of some importance, and a celebrated temple of Nemesis, who was sometimes called *Rhamnusia virgo.* The orator Antipho was born there.

aiebat. Cf. 38 note.

932. **quid eam tum?** sc. *esse aibat.*

quoiam. Cf. 763 note.

934. **qui,** 'on what grounds?'

noram et scio, 'I knew him and can vouch for it.'

936. **post illa,** or *postilla* = *postea,* occurs rarely and only in ante-Augustan writers. Cf. Phor. 347, 1018.

937. **quid illo sit factum.** Cf. 614 note.

939. **ne.** Cf. 324 note.

940-1. **scrupulus,** lit. 'a small pointed stone,' hence, 'anxiety, doubt, uneasiness.' Cf. Phor. 1019, Adel. 228 *inieci scrupulum homini.* A neuter form *scrupulum* or *scripulum* is used as the smallest division of weight, $\frac{1}{24}$ of an ounce.

dignus es cum tua religione, odium. This is the reading of A, C, P, and it was accepted by Donatus: other MSS. read *odio.* If *odium* be correct, an aposiopesis may be understood and *odium* taken as a vocative = *odiose homo,* 'you wretch, you deserve . . .' *Odium,* like *scelus,* is used in this sense by Plautus, Terence, and Cicero, e.g. Cic. Phil. 14. 3. 8 *Antonius, insigne odium omnium hominum vel deorum.*

cum tua religione = 'with your scruples.'

nodum in scirpo quaeris, lit. 'you are looking for a knot in a bulrush,' i.e. you are trying to find a difficulty where there is none. The proverb is also found in Pl. Men. 2. 1. 22, Ennius ap. Fest. p. 330, 7.

943. **id quaero,** 'I am trying to remember it.' Crito's difficulty in recalling names, cf. 928, is a happy touch of nature.

945. **Pasiphilast.** The MSS. reading *Pasibulast* is against the metre, while the dramatic propriety of making Πάμ-φιλος and Πασι-φίλη fall in love would be almost sufficient justification in itself for Fleckeisen's emendation, which has been adopted in the text.

947. **te credo credere.** For a similar expression cf. 958.

948. **redduxit.** Translate ' the event itself has reconciled me.'
 dudum. Cf. 582 note.
 o lepidum patrem, ' O best of fathers.' *Lepidus* is often used by Plautus and Terence, as applied to persons = ' charming,' to speech = ' smart,' ' clever.' Cf. Adel. 966 *o lepidum caput*, Pl. Trin. 809 *lepidast illa causa*.

950. **nempe** . . . 'I suppose' . . . **scilicet,** ' of course.'
 id. Pamphilus accompanies the word with a gesture of counting money. Simo and Chremes both understand this at once.

953. **non potest,** ' impossible.' Cf. 327 note.

954. **aliud magis ex sese et maius,** 'something else which concerns him more nearly, and is of greater importance to him.'

955. **non recte.** An instance of ἀμφιβολία or play upon words. Pamphilus means 'not justly,' Simo chooses to take it as ' not upright.' Cf. 863.

Act V. Scene 5.

Charinus overhears Pamphilus philosophising on his good-fortune, and cannot make out what has happened.

957. **proviso,** 'I am coming out to see.'
 eccum. Cf. 532 note.

958. The sense is, ' some people might suppose this too good to believe, but I want to believe it ' (and so I do).

959. **ēāpropter** is also used by Lucretius.

960. **propriae.** Cf. 716 note.

961. **aegritudo,** ' vexation.'

964. A notable instance of alliteration.
 solide, cf. 647 note.
 gaudia is a cognate accusative after *gavisurum*. Cf. 362.

Act V. Scene 6.

Davos appears, very sore from his punishment, but is pleased to hear how well matters have turned out. Pamphilus promises to use his influence with Chremes on behalf of Charinus, and both go into Glycerium's house, where, as Davos assures the audience, everything that remains will be done in proper form.

In the false ending Chremes promises Philumena to the faithful Charinus with a dowry of six talents.

967. et quidem ego, sc. *scio*.

more hominum, 'as usual;' cf. Pl. Trin. 1031 seqq.

sum nanctus. The MSS. have *sim*; but the difficulty of *sim* is so great and the alteration to *sum* so slight that we have followed the example of most editors in adopting the latter.

970. pater, sc. of Glycerium.

972. solus est quem diligant di. Bentley against all the MSS. reads *solus es quem diligunt di*, cf. Phor. 854 *nam sine controversia ab dis solus diligere, Antipho*. Others, reading *est*, suppose that Davos thus intimates that the child has died. But such hypotheses are quite unnecessary. What more natural than that Davos should flatter his young master by an extravagant compliment on his infant son and heir? And the congratulation was not without reason. A match, against a father's will, with an unknown and almost penniless girl, was likely enough to have brought both Pamphilus and his family to ruin. Now his son would have an acknowledged and honourable position, with the prospect of a handsome property. Translate, 'he is to be the only favourite of the gods.' The way in which Davos cuts short his young master's threatened rhapsody on the baby is characteristic enough.

974. in tempore ipso. Cf. 532 note.

mi. It is better to consider *mi* as a *dat. commodi*, 'at the very nick of time for me,' rather than as after *advenis*. No certain instance of a dative after *advenio* occurs in a classical author.

977. atque adeo. Cf. 532 note.

980. intus despondebitur, 'the betrothal (of Charinus and Philumena) will take place within.' The Cistellaria and Casina of Plautus end in a similar way.

981. plaudite. Between the first and second acts of a Roman comedy it was the custom to introduce a lyrical monologue (*canticum*) with a flute accompaniment. Sometimes, as in the Trinummus, this *canticum* was made an integral part of the play, but more commonly it was performed by a *cantor*, who also came forward at the end of a play and said to the audience '*plaudite;*' cf. Hor. A. P. 155 *donec cantor 'vos plaudite' dicat*. In all Terence's plays the MSS. mark the *cantor* by Ω. The actors are often indicated by letters of the Greek alphabet; the *cantor*, therefore, who appeared at the end of all, is indicated by the last letter.

ALTER EXITUS.

In a few of the later MSS. a second ending, twenty-one lines in length, is found. This ending was known to Donatus and Eugraphius, and is certainly of considerable antiquity. Wagner thinks it possible that it may have been the original ending, but that Terence afterwards altered it on finding that the audience showed little interest in the fortunes of Charinus. It seems however far more likely to have been the addition of some later critic who thought the play incomplete without a definite settlement of the second pair of lovers. There are considerable corruptions and omissions in the text; the language in more than one place is involved and obscure, though Ritschl, whose emendations have been generally adopted, has spent on the elucidation of this passage more trouble than perhaps it deserves.

(977–8). Ritschl suggested these lines as a connecting link.

983. **alterae** for *alterius*. A dat. fem. sing. *alterae* is found Haut. 271 : cf. 608 note.

985. **sors tollitur**, 'the lot is being drawn.'

986. 'The match to which you refer is not new to me :' i.e. Chremes had known that Charinus wished to marry Philumena, but had entertained other designs for her.

989–90. 'But I was anxious that our friendship, which has been handed down to us by our fathers, should undiminished be handed on to our children.'

amicitia nostra = friendship of Chremes and Simo. The text as it stands is an anacoluthon, *amicitia* being a *Nominativus pendens*. We should have expected *amicitiam nostram . . . nulla parte abducta*.

992. **detur**, sc. *Philumena Charino*.

994–7. These lines are very corrupt. If Ritschl's emendations be adopted the sense may be as follows : ' What shall I say? For to have found you as well disposed towards me as before, gives me no less pleasure than now to obtain what I seek from you.' It is hard to believe that a passage so awkward and involved came from the pen of Terence.

997–8. 'When you, sc. Charinus, have devoted yourself to him, sc. Chremes, as henceforth will be your aim, do you form your opinion.'

999. **alienus**, 'estranged,' sc. owing to the matrimonial schemes of Chremes.

1000. 'You may guess that to be true from my case,' i.e. Chremes knew only too much about him and his doings.

INDEX TO NOTES.

(References are to the number of the lines. Words distinguished by an asterisk are ἅπαξ λεγόμενα. Words enclosed in brackets are emendations, or of doubtful authority. When the same word has been noted more than once, but in different case, person, tense, etc., the references will be found under the form which occurs first.)

abiret, 175, 344.
Ablative *(after* facio, fio), 614, 709, 937.
— *(of price)*, 369.
abs, 489.
abutitur, 5.
Accusative *(of exclamation)*, 604, 869, 876, 948, 956.
— *(of kindred meaning)*, 964.
— *(of limitation or respect)*, 45, 162, 289, 376, 414, 448, 738.
— *(peculiar uses of)*, 5, 58, 157, 307.
Accusative and Infinitive in indignant questions, 245.
actumst, 465.
ad *(with Acc. = Gen.)*, 138, 320, 482.
ad erum iurandum, 728.
adeo, 162, 415, 440, 532, 579, 585, 757, 759, 775, 879.
adiuro, 694.
adlegatum, 899.
adparetur, 594.
adplicat se, 924.
adponi, 331.
adprime, 61.
adpulit, 1, 807.
*adtemperate, 916.
advesperascit, 581.
advorser, 263.
advorsum, 42, 265.
Aediles Curules, note on title.

aegre ferens, 137.
agis, 186, 415, 708, 713.
alere, 57.
alias, 529.
alienus, 999.
aliquot, 534.
Alliteration, 671, 691, 964.
*altercasti, 653.
alterae, 983.
ambis, 373.
amentium haud amantium, 218.
amolimini, 707.
ἀμφιβολία, 955.
an, 621, 807.
Anacoluthon, 989–90.
animum adiungant, 56.
annona, 746.
ante eamus, 536.
antea, 52.
antiquom obtines, 817.
ἅπαξ λεγόμενα, 232, 265, 653, 688, 814, 916.
aperiunt se, 632.
apiscier, 332.
Apollinis responsum, 698.
Aposiopesis, 607, 803.
apud, 254.
ara, 726.
argumentum, 6.
ars, 31, 33.
Assonance, 378, 691.
Asyndeton, 161, 248, 304, 373, 676, 680.

at, 666.
atque, 225, 607, 698.
attat, 125.
attentus, 303.
attigas, 789.
Attraction (inverse), 3, 26.

bona verba, 204.

callide, 201.
canes ad venandum, 57.
cantor, 981.
carnufex, 183.
catus, 855.
cautiost, 400.
Chremes (*declension of*), 247.
circuitione, 202.
clam, 287.
claudier, 573.
cognatorum, 71.
commerui, 139.
commoveat, 280.
commutaturum, 410.
complacita, 645.
* compotrix, 232.
concludar, 386.
concrepuit, 682.
confecit, 650.
confidens, 855.
confore, 167.
conieci, 602, 620, 667.
Constructio κατὰ σύνεσιν, 250, 607, 627, 745.
consuetudine, 560.
contaminari, 16.
convenere, 13.
coram, 490.
credo (*parenthetical*), 313, 673.
curentur, 30.

damnum, 143.
dari bibere, 484.
dari verba, 505.
Dative (*of advantage*), 331, 490, 528, 905, 974.
— (*of complement*), 8.
— (*ethic*), 842.
decrerat, 238.

dedere sese, 63.
dehinc, 22, 190.
deludier, 203.
despondi, 102, 980.
di vostram fidem, 716.
dictum ac factum, 381.
dieculam, 710.
differat, 408.
disputant, 15.
dixti, 621.
drachumis, 451.
dudum, 582, 824.
duint, 666.
dum, 329, 677.
-dum (*enclitic*), 29.
duriter, 74.

ea gratia, 433, 587.
ecastor, 486.
eccum, 532, 580, 855, 957.
edepol, 305.
effertur, 117.
ei = hei, 73, 302.
Ellipse, 29, 30, 31, 33, 82, 149, 226, 237, 263, 300, 336, 343, 344, 345, 347, 348, 361, 373, 381, 400, 409, 416, 494, 500, 533, 635, 642, 663, 683, 712, 716, 804, 807, 817, 853, 868, 883, 893, 907, 928.
ellum, 855.
em, 604.
emersurum, 562.
enicas, 660.
enim, 91, 503, 823, 848.
enimvero, 91, 206.
ephebis, 51.
eradicent, 761.
ergo, 711, 850.
erilem filium, 602.
etiam, 116, 201, 503.
euge, 345.
ex, 37.
ex sese, 954.
exanimatus, 131.
excessis, 760.
excidit (uxore), 423.

exigendae, 27.
expostulem, 639.
exprobratio, 44.

fabula, 747, 925.
face, 680, 712, 821.
facere (*with Abl.*), 614, 709, 937.
facile, 720.
factum, 44.
falso, 505, 647.
familiariter, 111, 136.
fatetur, 14.
favete, 24.
faxis, 753, 854.
fecit = dixit, 178.
fide, 296, 716.
foras, 580.
fortem, 445.
frequens, 107.
fugin, 337.
furcifer, 618.
futtili, 609.
Future Perfect (*use of*), 854, 892.

Genitive (*in* -î *for* -ii), 2.
— (*in* -i, -ae *for* -ius), 608, 983.
— (*in* -i *for* -ûs), 365.
— (*partitive*), 2, 70.
genium, 289.
*grandiuscula, 814.

habeo gratiam, 42.
habet, 83.
haec = hae, 328.
Hiatus, 264, 345, 616, 665, 769, 817.
hic (δεικτικῶς), 310, 650, 691, 787.
— (*of time*), 389, 720.

ibi, 356, 379.
ibi tum, 106, 131, 223.
id, 162, 414, 535, 950.
id negoti, 2, 521.
idoneus, 492.
igitur, 519.
ilico, 514.
illi = illic, 745.

illo = illuc, 362.
Imperfect (*in* -ibam), 38.
— (*Subj. for Pluperf.*), 793.
immo, 629.
in eo, 15, 94.
in mora, 424, 467.
in portu navigo, 480.
in proclivi, 701.
in rem, 546.
in tempore, 532, 758, 974.
in vado, 845.
in viam, 190.
in (*with Acc. to express purpose*), 369.
Indicative (*noteworthy uses of*), 45, 311, 315, 329, 372, 422, 488, 517, 536, 559, 569, 622, 650, 714, 771, 849, 918.
indignum facinus, 145.
induxti, 572.
Infinitive (*archaic in* -ier), 203, 332, 573.
— (*after* video), 580.
— (*for Gerund*), 57.
— (*Historic*), 62, 97, 369, 662.
— (*in indignant questions*), 245, 689.
— (*Pres. for Fut.*), 379, 411, 613.
ingeniis, 93, 275.
iniuria, 60, 156, 214.
inludatis, 758, 822.
inmemores discipuli, 477.
inmutatum, 242.
inpotenti, 879.
instat factum, 147.
*integrascit, 688.
integro, 26.
intellegit, 4.
interminatus, 496.
interturbat, 663.
inventum dabo, 683, 684, 703, 864.
invenustus, 245.
iocularium, 782.
ipsus, 360.
istaec, 501, 565.
ita, 11, 65, 492, 643, 849.

lactasses, 648, 912.
lavet, 483.
lepidum. 948.
liberali, 561.
liquido, 729.
Ludis Megalensibus, note on title.

magister, 54.
malitia, 723.
malle melius, 427.
malum, 431, 640.
manibus pedibusque, 161, 676.
matronam, 364.
meditatus, 406.
minuere, 392.
missum face, 680, 833.
modo, 594.
modo ut, 409.
modum, 95.
more hominum, 967.
morem gessero, 641.

nam, 51.
nanctus sum, 967.
ne (*surely*), 324.
ne (*after* dum), 902.
— (*with Imperative*), 384, 543, 868.
— quid nimis, 61.
nĕ = nonne, 17, 495, 504.
necessus, 372.
nescio qui. 841.
nil quicquam, 90.
nisi si, 249.
nolo (*with Subj.*), 819.
non = nē, 787.
nonne, 238.
nullus, 370, 599, 608.
numquidnam, 235.
nunciam, 171.
nuncine, 683.

obsonatum. 451.
ob (*with Acc.* = *Gen.*), 138.
ocius, 724.
odium, 941.

omine, 200.
operam do (*with Acc.*), 157.
optato, 533.
optume, 335, 593.
opus, 728, 738, 740.
opus facto, 490, 715.
opus parato, 523.
oratione, 12, 141.
oscitantis, 181.
Oxymoron, 17.

Paronomasia, 42, 218.
parvolo, 35.
Pasiphila, 945.
paucis [verbis], 29.
paulo, 266.
paululum, 360.
pedisequas, 123.
per, 538, 834.
per tempus, 783.
percussit. 125.
Perfect Subj. (*for Imperf.*), 914.
perii, 213, 591.
Perinthiam, 9.
* peropus, 265.
perscitus, 486.
philosophos, 57.
Philumenam, 306.
pistrinum, 214, 600.
platea, 796.
plaudite, 981.
Pleonasm, 90, 106, 201, 239.
plerique, 55.
poeta, 1, 7.
pol, 459.
Polysyndeton, 676.
porro, 22.
possiet, 874.
post illa, 936.
potest (*impersonal*), 327, 691, 861, 953.
praescripsti, 151.
[premit]. 633.
Present Tense (*expressing energy*), 594.
pretium, 39.
primum, 156.

INDEX TO NOTES. 127

prius, 27.
pro, 237, 732.
pro deum fidem, 237.
pro servitio, 675.
processit, 671.
prodat, 313.
prodeo, 115.
profer, 329.
Prolepsis, 792.
promoveo, 711.
proprium, 716.
propulsabo, 395.
prorsus, 510.
Proverbial expressions, 61, 126, 161, 164, 636, 941.
providentur, 208.
proviso, 957.

quadrupedem constringito, 865.
quam, 136.
quî, 6, 148, 334.
quid ais? 137, 184, 301, 517, 575.
quid hominum, 745.
quid istic, 572.
quin, 45, 704.
quod (*construction of*), 45.
quod si, 258, 604.
quoium, 763, 932.
quom, 1, 488, 517, 622, 771.
quor, 48.
quorsum, 264.

recta via, 442, 600.
recte, 955.
redducunt, 559.
relicuom, 25.
religio, 730, 941.
resipisco, 698.
re uxoria, 829.
reviso, 404.
Rhamnusium, 930.
ridiculum caput, 371.

sane, 195.
Scansion (*peculiarities of*), 5, 23, 25, 42, 43, 52, 91, 125, 171,
206, 237, 242, 301, 302, 345, 391, 437, 443, 465, 474, 483, 628, 702, 708, 760, 796.
scire *or* sciri, 337.
scirpo, 941.
scribundis, 5.
scrupulus, 940.
se (*omitted before Infin.*), 14.
semper, 175.
servibas, 38.
setius, 507.
sic, 804.
sicine, 689.
siet, 234, 288, 390, 408, 424, 454.
sin, 165.
sine omni, 391.
sis sciens, 508, 775.
sive = vel si, 190.
sobrinus, 801.
solidum, 647.
solus est quem diligant di, 972.
spectatum, 91.
stilo, 12.
Subjunctive (*after causal relative*), 664, 749.
— (*co-ordinate with Indic.*), 273, 536, 649.
— (*deliberative*), 613, 639.
— (*in questions*), 191, 282, 499, 584, 649, 915.
— (*noteworthy uses of*), 263, 310, 376, 390, 395, 454, 618, 619, 622, 625.
— (*potential*), 53, 135, 203, 460, 489, 619, 814.
sublimem, 861.
substet, 914.
successit, 670.
suffarcinatam, 770.
sycophantam, 815.
symbolam, 88.
Syncopated forms, 151, 500, 506, 518, 572, 593, 621, 760, 882, 883.
Synizesis, 22, 25, 42, 64, 93, 95, 202, 210, 237, 263, 390, 408, 457, 541, 557, 781, 814, 959.

tandem, 492.
temporibus, 475.
teneo, 300, 498.
tetulissem, 808, 832.
tibiis paribus, note on title.
Tmesis, 63, 263, 455, 486.
tollere, 219.
tulit, 188.
tum, 926.
tute, 500.

ubi ubi, 684.
ulcisci, 624.
ultro, 100.
unam, 118.
usque, 303.
usque ad necem, 199.
ὕστερον πρότερον, 841.
ut ne = ne, 259, 327, 834.

ut ne = ut non, 699.
utiquam, 330.

valeant, 696.
vecordia, 625.
vel, 489, 680.
[verae], 103.
Verbal Substantive, 44.
verbenas, 726.
verentur, 638.
verus, 423, 629.
veterator, 457.
via, 442.
viciniae, 70.
vide, 350, 399, 588.
viso, 535.
volgus servorum, 583.

Zeugma, 624.

THE END.

September, 1885.

BOOKS

PRINTED AT

The Clarendon Press, Oxford,

AND PUBLISHED FOR THE UNIVERSITY BY

HENRY FROWDE,

AT THE OXFORD UNIVERSITY PRESS WAREHOUSE,
AMEN CORNER, LONDON.

LEXICONS, GRAMMARS, &c.

A Greek-English Lexicon, by Henry George Liddell, D.D., and Robert Scott D.D. *Seventh Edition.* 1883. 4to. *cloth*, 1*l.* 16*s.*

A Greek-English Lexicon, abridged from the above, chiefly for the use of Schools. 1883. square 12mo. *cloth*, 7*s.* 6*d.*

Graecae Grammaticae Rudimenta in usum Scholarum. Auctore Carolo Wordsworth, D.C.L. *Nineteenth Edition*, 1882. 12mo. *cloth*, 4*s.*

A Latin Dictionary, founded on Andrews' Edition of Freund's Latin Dictionary. Revised, enlarged, and in great part re-written, by Charlton T. Lewis, Ph.D., and Charles Short, LL.D. 4to. *cloth*, 1*l.* 5*s.*

A Practical Grammar of the Sanskrit Language, arranged with reference to the Classical Languages of Europe, for the use of English Students. By Monier Williams, M.A. *Fourth Edition.* 8vo. *cloth*, 15*s.*

An Icelandic-English Dictionary, based on the MS. collections of the late R. Cleasby. Enlarged and completed by G. Vigfusson. 4to *cloth*, 3*l.* 7*s.*

An Anglo-Saxon Dictionary, based on the MS. collections of the late Joseph Bosworth, D.D. Edited and enlarged by Professor T. N. Toller, M.A., Owens College, Manchester. Parts I and II, each 15*s.* *To be completed in four Parts.*

An Etymological Dictionary of the English Language, arranged on an Historical basis. By W. W. Skeat, M.A. *Second Edition.* 4to. *cloth*, 2*l.* 4*s.*

A Supplement to the First Edition of the above. 4to. 2*s.* 6*d.*

A Concise Etymological Dictionary of the English Language. By W. W Skeat. M.A. Crown 8vo. *cloth*, 5*s.* 6*d.*

A New English Dictionary, on Historical Principles, founded mainly on the materials collected by the Philological Society. Edited by James A. H. Murray, LL.D., President of the Philological Society; with the assistance of many Scholars and men of Science. Part I. A—ANT (pp. xvi, 352). Imperial 4to. 12*s.* 6*d.*

Books lately printed at the

GREEK CLASSICS.

Aeschylus: Tragoediae et Fragmenta, ex recensione Guil. Dindorfii. *Second Edition*, 1851. 8vo. *cloth*, 5s. 6d.

Sophocles: Tragoediae et Fragmenta, ex recensione et cum commentariis Guil. Dindorfii. *Third Edition*, 2 vols. fcap. 8vo. *cloth*, 1l. 1s. Each Play separately, *limp*, 2s. 6d.

    The Text alone, printed on writing paper, with large margin, royal 16mo. *cloth*, 8s.

    The Text alone, square 16mo. *cloth*, 3s. 6d.

    Each Play separately, *limp*, 6d. (See also page 11.)

Sophocles: Tragoediae et Fragmenta, cum Annotatt. Guil. Dindorfii. Tomi II. 1849. 8vo. *cloth*, 10s.

    The Text, Vol. I. 5s. 6d. The Notes, Vol. II. 4s. 6d.

Euripides: Tragoediae et Fragmenta, ex recensione Guil. Dindorfii. Tomi II. 1834. 8vo. *cloth*, 10s.

Aristophanes: Comoediae et Fragmenta, ex recensione Guil. Dindorfii. Tomi II. 1835. 8vo. *cloth*, 11s.

Aristoteles; ex recensione Immanuelis Bekkeri. Accedunt Indices Sylburgiani. Tomi XI. 1837. 8vo. *cloth*, 2l. 10s.

    The volumes may be had separately (except Vol. IX.), 5s. 6d. each.

Aristotelis Ethica Nicomachea, ex recensione Immanuelis Bekkeri. Crown 8vo. *cloth*, 5s.

Demosthenes: ex recensione Guil. Dindorfii. Tomi IV. 1846. 8vo. *cloth*, 1l. 1s.

Homerus: Ilias, ex rec. Guil. Dindorfii. 8vo. *cloth*, 5s. 6d.

Homerus: Odyssea, ex rec. Guil. Dindorfii. 1855. 8vo. *cloth*, 5s. 6d.

Plato: The Apology, with a revised Text and English Notes, and a Digest of Platonic Idioms, by James Riddell, M.A. 1878. 8vo. *cloth*, 8s. 6d.

Plato: Philebus, with a revised Text and English Notes, by Edward Poste, M.A. 1860. 8vo. *cloth*, 7s. 6d.

Plato: Sophistes and Politicus, with a revised Text and English Notes, by L. Campbell, M.A. 1867. 8vo. *cloth*, 18s.

Plato: Theaetetus, with a revised Text and English Notes, by L. Campbell, M.A. *Second Edition.* 8vo. *cloth*, 10s. 6d.

Plato: The Dialogues, translated into English, with Analyses and Introductions. By B. Jowett, M.A. *A new Edition in five volumes.* 1875. Medium 8vo. *cloth*, 3l. 10s.

Plato: The Republic, translated into English, with an Analysis and Introduction. By B. Jowett, M.A. Medium 8vo. *cloth*, 12s. 6d.

Thucydides: translated into English, with Introduction, Marginal Analysis, Notes and Indices. By the same. 2 vols. 1881. Medium 8vo. *cloth*, 1l. 12s.

THE HOLY SCRIPTURES.

The Holy Bible in the Earliest English Versions, made from the Latin Vulgate by John Wycliffe and his followers: edited by the Rev. J. Forshall and Sir F. Madden. 4 vols. 1850. royal 4to. *cloth*, 3*l*. 3*s*.

Also reprinted from the above, with Introduction and Glossary by W. W. SKEAT, M.A.

(1) **The New Testament** in English, according to the Version by John Wycliffe, about A.D. 1380, and Revised by John Purvey, about A.D. 1388. 1879. Extra fcap. 8vo. *cloth*, 6*s*.

(2) **The Book of Job, Psalms, Proverbs, Ecclesiastes,** and Solomon's Song, according to the Version by John Wycliffe. Revised by John Purvey. Extra fcap. 8vo. *cloth*, 3*s*. 6*d*.

The Holy Bible: an exact reprint, page for page, of the Authorized Version published in the year 1611. Demy 4to. *half bound*, 1*l*. 1*s*.

Novum Testamentum Graece. Edidit Carolus Lloyd, S.T.P.R., necnon Episcopus Oxoniensis. 18mo. *cloth*, 3*s*.

The same on writing paper, small 4to. *cloth*, 10*s*. 6*d*.

Novum Testamentum Graece juxta Exemplar Millianum. 18mo. *cloth*, 2*s*. 6*d*.

The same on writing paper, small 4to. *cloth*, 9*s*.

The Greek Testament, with the Readings adopted by the Revisers of the Authorised Version:—
- (1) Pica type. *Second Edition, with Marginal References.* Demy 8vo. *cloth*, 10*s*. 6*d*.
- (2) Long Primer type. Fcap. 8vo. *cloth*, 4*s*. 6*d*.
- (3) The same, on writing paper, with wide margin, *cloth*, 15*s*.

Evangelia Sacra Graece. fcap. 8vo. *limp*, 1*s*. 6*d*.

Vetus Testamentum ex Versione Septuaginta Interpretum secundum exemplar Vaticanum Romae editum. Accedit potior varietas Codicis Alexandrini. *Editio Altera.* Tomi III. 1875. 18mo. *cloth*, 18*s*.

The Oxford Bible for Teachers, containing supplementary HELPS TO THE STUDY OF THE BIBLE, including summaries of the several Books, with copious explanatory notes; and Tables illustrative of Scripture History and the characteristics of Bible Lands with a complete Index of Subjects, a Concordance, a Dictionary of Proper Names, and a series of Maps. Prices in various sizes and bindings from 3*s*. to 2*l*. 5*s*.

Helps to the Study of the Bible, taken from the OXFORD BIBLE FOR TEACHERS, comprising summaries of the several Books with copious explanatory Notes and Tables illustrative of Scripture History and the characteristics of Bible Lands; with a complete Index of Subjects, a Concordance, a Dictionary of Proper Names, and a series of Maps. Crown 8vo. *cloth*, 3*s*. 6*d*., 16mo. *cloth*, 1*s*.

ECCLESIASTICAL HISTORY, &c.

Baedae Historia Ecclesiastica. Edited, with English Notes, by G. H. Moberly, M.A. Crown 8vo. *cloth*, 10s. 6d.

Chapters of Early English Church History. By William Bright, D.D. 8vo. *cloth*, 12s.

Eusebius' Ecclesiastical History, according to the Text of Burton. With an Introduction by William Bright, D.D. Crown 8vo. *cloth*, 8s. 6d.

Socrates' Ecclesiastical History, according to the Text of Hussey. With an Introduction by William Bright, D.D. Crown 8vo. *cloth*, 7s. 6d.

ENGLISH THEOLOGY.

Butler's Analogy, with an Index. 8vo. *cloth*, 5s. 6d.

Butler's Sermons. 8vo. *cloth*, 5s. 6d.

Hooker's Works, with his Life by Walton, arranged by John Keble, M.A. *Sixth Edition*, 3 vols. 1874. 8vo. *cloth*, 1l. 11s. 6d.

Hooker's Works; the text as arranged by John Keble, M.A. 2 vols. 1875. 8vo. *cloth*, 11s.

Pearson's Exposition of the Creed. Revised and corrected by E. Burton, D.D. *Sixth Edition*, 1877. 8vo. *cloth*, 10s. 6d.

Waterland's Review of the Doctrine of the Eucharist, with a Preface by the late Bishop of London. Crown 8vo. *cloth*, 6s. 6d.

ENGLISH HISTORY.

A History of England. Principally in the Seventeenth Century. By Leopold Von Ranke. 6 vols. 8vo. *cloth*, 3l. 3s.

Clarendon's (Edw. Earl of) History of the Rebellion and Civil Wars in England. To which are subjoined the Notes of Bishop Warburton. 7 vols. 1849. medium 8vo. *cloth*, 2l. 10s.

Clarendon's (Edw. Earl of) History of the Rebellion and Civil Wars in England. 7 vols. 1839. 18mo. *cloth*, 1l. 1s.

Freeman's (E. A.) History of the Norman Conquest of England: its Causes and Results. *In Six Volumes.* 8vo. *cloth*, 5l. 9s. 6d.
    Vol. I. and II. together, *Third Edition*, 1877. 1l. 16s.
    Vol. III. *Second Edition*, 1874. 1l. 1s.
    Vol. IV. *Second Edition*, 1875. 1l. 1s.
    Vol. V. 1876. 1l. 1s.
    Vol. VI. Index, 1879. 10s. 6d.

Rogers's History of Agriculture and Prices in England, A.D. 1259—1793. Vols. I. and II. (1259—1400). 8vo. *cloth*, 2l. 2s.
    Vols. III. and IV. (1401-1582). 8vo. *cloth*, 2l. 10s.

Clarendon Press Series.

I. ENGLISH.

A First Reading Book. By Marie Eichens of Berlin; and edited by Anne J. Clough. Ext. fcap. 8vo. *stiff covers*, 4d.

Oxford Reading Book, Part I. For Little Children. Ext. fcap. 8vo. *stiff covers*, 6d.

Oxford Reading Book, Part II. For Junior Classes. Ext. fcap. 8vo. *stiff covers*, 6d.

An Elementary English Grammar and Exercise Book. By O. W. Tancock, M.A. *Second Edition.* Ext. fcap. 8vo. 1s. 6d.

An English Grammar and Reading Book, for Lower Forms in Classical Schools. By the same Author. *Fourth Edition.* Ext. fcap. 8vo. *cloth*, 3s. 6d.

Typical Selections from the best English Writers, with Introductory Notices. In Two Volumes. Extra fcap. 8vo. *cloth*, 3s. 6d. each.

The Philology of the English Tongue. By J. Earle, M.A., formerly Fellow of Oriel College, and Professor of Anglo-Saxon, Oxford. *Third Edition.* Ext. fcap. 8vo. *cloth*, 7s. 6d.

A Book for Beginners in Anglosaxon. By John Earle, M.A. *Third Edition.* Extra fcap. 8vo. *cloth*, 2s. 6d.

An Anglo-Saxon Primer, with Grammar, Notes, and Glossary. By Henry Sweet, M.A. *Second Edition.* Extra fcap. 8vo. *cloth*, 2s. 6d.

An Anglo-Saxon Reader, in Prose and Verse, with Grammatical Introduction, Notes, and Glossary. By Henry Sweet, M.A. *Fourth Edition.* Extra fcap. 8vo. *cloth*, 8s. 6d.

First Middle English Primer; with Grammar and Glossary. By Henry Sweet, M.A. Extra fcap. 8vo. *cloth*, 2s.

The Ormulum; with the Notes and Glossary of Dr. R. M. White. Edited by R. Holt, M.A. 2 vols. Extra fcap. 8vo. *cloth*, 21s.

Specimens of Early English. A New and Revised Edition. With Introduction, Notes, and Glossarial Index. By R. Morris, LL.D., and W. W. Skeat, M.A.
 Part I. From Old English Homilies to King Horn (A.D. 1150 to A.D. 1300). Extra fcap. 8vo. *cloth*, 9s.
 Part II. From Robert of Gloucester to Gower (A.D. 1298 to A.D. 1393). Extra fcap. 8vo. *cloth*, 7s. 6d.

Specimens of English Literature, from the 'Ploughmans Crede' to the 'Shepheardes Calender' (A.D. 1394 to A.D. 1579). With Introduction, Notes, and Glossarial Index. By W. W. Skeat, M.A. *Third Edition.* Ext. fcap. 8vo. *cloth*, 7s. 6d.

The Vision of William concerning Piers the Plowman, by William Langland. Edited, with Notes, by W. W. Skeat, M.A. *Third Edition.* Ext. fcap. 8vo. *cloth*, 4s. 6d.

Chaucer. The Prioresses Tale; Sire Thopas; The Monkes Tale; The Clerkes Tale; The Squieres Tale, &c. Edited by W. W. Skeat, M.A. *Second Edition.* Ext. fcap. 8vo. *cloth*, 4s. 6d.

Chaucer. The Tale of the Man of Lawe; The Par-
doneres Tale; The Second Nonnes Tale; The Chanouns Yemannes Tale.
By the same Editor. *Second Edition.* Extra fcap. 8vo. *cloth,* 4s. 6d.

The Tale of Gamelyn. Edited, with Notes and a Glossarial Index, by W. W. Skeat, M.A. Extra fcap. 8vo. *stiff covers,* 1s. 6d.

Old English Drama. Marlowe's Tragical History of Doctor
Faustus, and Greene's Honourable History of Friar Bacon and Friar Bungay.
Edited by A. W. Ward, M.A. Extra fcap. 8vo. *cloth,* 5s. 6d.

Marlowe. Edward II. With Notes, &c. By O. W.
Tancock, M.A., Head Master of Norwich School. Extra fcap. 8vo. *cloth,* 3s.

Shakespeare. Hamlet. Edited by W. G. Clark, M.A., and
W. Aldis Wright, M.A. Extra fcap. 8vo. *stiff covers,* 2s.

Shakespeare. Select Plays. Edited by W. Aldis Wright,
M.A. Extra fcap. 8vo. *stiff covers.*
    The Tempest, 1s. 6d.   King Lear, 1s. 6d.
    As You Like It, 1s. 6d.   A Midsummer Night's Dream, 1s. 6d.
    Julius Cæsar, 2s.   Coriolanus, 2s. 6d.
    Richard the Third, 2s. 6d.   Henry the Fifth, 2s.
        Twelfth Night, 1s. 6d.

Milton. Areopagitica. With Introduction and Notes. By
J. W. Hales, M.A. *Third Edition.* Extra fcap. 8vo. *cloth,* 3s.

Milton. Samson Agonistes. Edited with Introduction
and Notes by John Churton Collins. Extra fcap. 8vo. *stiff covers,* 1s.

Bunyan. Holy War. Edited by E. Venables, M.A. *In
the Press.* (See also p. 7.)

Addison. Selections from Papers in the Spectator. With
Notes. By T. Arnold, M.A., University College. Extra fcap. 8vo. *cloth,* 4s. 6d.

**Burke. Four Letters on the Proposals for Peace with
the Regicide Directory of France.** Edited, with Introduction
and Notes, by E. J. Payne, M.A. Extra fcap. 8vo. *cloth,* 5s. *See also page* 7.

Also the following in paper covers.

Goldsmith. Deserted Village. 2d.

Gray. Selected Poems. Edited by Edmund Gosse, Clark
Lecturer in English Literature at the University of Cambridge. Extra fcap.
8vo. *stiff covers,* 1s. 6d.; *bound in white parchment,* 3s.

Gray. Elegy, and Ode on Eton College. 2d.

Johnson. Vanity of Human Wishes. With Notes by E. J.
Payne, M.A. 4d.

Keats. Hyperion, Book I. With Notes by W. T. Arnold, 4d.

Milton. With Notes by R. C. Browne, M.A.
    Lycidas, 3d.   L'Allegro, 3d.   Il Penseroso, 4d.
    Comus, 6d.   Samson Agonistes, 6d.

Parnell. The Hermit. 2d.

Scott. Lay of the Last Minstrel. Introduction and Canto I.
With Notes by W. Minto, M.A. 6d.

Clarendon Press Series. 7

A SERIES OF ENGLISH CLASSICS

Designed to meet the wants of Students in English Literature; by the late J. S. BREWER, M.A., Professor of English Literature at King's College, London.

1. **Chaucer.** The Prologue to the Canterbury Tales; The Knightes Tale; The Nonne Prestes Tale. Edited by R. Morris, LL.D. *Fifty-first Thousand.* Extra fcap. 8vo. *cloth*, 2s. 6d. See also p. 6.

2. **Spenser's Faery Queene.** Books I and II. By G. W. Kitchin, M.A. Extra fcap. 8vo. *cloth*, 2s. 6d. each.

3. **Hooker.** Ecclesiastical Polity, Book I. Edited by R. W. Church, M.A., Dean of St. Paul's. Extra fcap. 8vo. *cloth*, 2s.

4. **Shakespeare.** Select Plays. Edited by W. G. Clark, M.A., and W. Aldis Wright, M.A. Extra fcap. 8vo. *stiff covers.*
    I. The Merchant of Venice. 1s.   II. Richard the Second. 1s. 6d.
    III. Macbeth. 1s. 6d. (For other Plays, see p. 6.)

5. **Bacon.**
    I. Advancement of Learning. Edited by W. Aldis Wright, M.A. *Second Edition.* Extra fcap. 8vo. *cloth*, 4s. 6d.
    II. The Essays. With Introduction and Notes. *Preparing.*

6. **Milton.** Poems. Edited by R. C. Browne, M.A. In Two Volumes. *Fourth Edition.* Ext. fcap. 8vo. *cloth*, 6s. 6d.
    Sold separately, Vol. I. 4s., Vol. II. 3s.

7. **Dryden.** Stanzas on the Death of Oliver Cromwell; Astraea Redux; Annus Mirabilis; Absalom and Achitophel; Religio Laici; The Hind and the Panther. Edited by W. D. Christie, M.A., Trinity College, Cambridge. *Second Edition.* Extra fcap. 8vo. *cloth*, 3s. 6d.

8. **Bunyan.** The Pilgrim's Progress, Grace Abounding, and A Relation of his Imprisonment. Edited, with Biographical Introduction and Notes, by E. Venables, M.A., Precentor of Lincoln. Extra fcap. 8vo. *cloth*, 5s.

9. **Pope.** With Introduction and Notes. By Mark Pattison, B.D., Rector of Lincoln College, Oxford.
    I. Essay on Man. *Sixth Edition.* Extra fcap. 8vo. *stiff covers*, 1s. 6d.
    II. Satires and Epistles. *Second Edition.* Extra fcap. 8vo. *stiff covers*, 2s.

10. **Johnson.** Select Works. Lives of Dryden and Pope, and Rasselas. Edited by Alfred Milnes, B.A. (Lond.), late Scholar of Lincoln College, Oxford. Extra fcap. 8vo. *cloth*, 4s. 6d.

11. **Burke.** Edited, with Introduction and Notes, by E. J. Payne, M.A., Fellow of University College, Oxford.
    I. Thoughts on the Present Discontents; the Two Speeches on America, etc. *Second Edition.* Extra fcap. 8vo. *cloth*, 4s. 6d.
    II. Reflections on the French Revolution. *Second Edition.* Extra fcap. 8vo. *cloth*, 5s. *See also p.* 6.

12. **Cowper.** Edited, with Life, Introductions, and Notes, by H. T. Griffith, B.A., formerly Scholar of Pembroke College, Oxford.
    I. The Didactic Poems of 1782, with Selections from the Minor Pieces, A.D. 1779-1783. Ext. fcap. 8vo. *cloth*, 3s.
    II. The Task, with Tirocinium, and Selections from the Minor Poems, A.D. 1784-1799. Ext. fcap. 8vo. *cloth*, 3s.

II. LATIN.

Rudimenta Latina; comprising Accidence, and Exercises of a very Elementary Character, for the use of Beginners By John Barrow Allen, M.A. Extra fcap. 8vo. *cloth*, 2s. *Just Published.*

An Elementary Latin Grammar. By the same Author. *Third Edition.* Extra fcap. 8vo. *cloth*, 2s. 6d.

A First Latin Exercise Book. By the same Author. *Fourth Edition.* Extra fcap. 8vo. *cloth*, 2s. 6d.

A Second Latin Exercise Book. By the same Author. Extra fcap. 8vo. *cloth*, 3s. 6d.

Exercises in Latin Prose Composition. By G. G. Ramsay, M.A. Extra fcap. 8vo. *cloth*, 4s. 6d.

Reddenda Minora, or Easy Passages, Latin and Greek, for Unseen Translation. For the use of Lower Forms. Composed and selected by C. S. Jerram, M.A. Extra fcap. 8vo. *cloth*, 1s. 6d.

Anglice Reddenda, or Easy Extracts, Latin and Greek, for Unseen Translation. By C. S. Jerram, M.A. Extra fcap. 8vo. *cloth*, 2s. 6d.

Passages for Translation into Latin. Selected by J. Y. Sargent, M.A. *Sixth Edition.* Ext. fcap. 8vo. *cloth*, 2s. 6d.

First Latin Reader. By T. J. Nunns, M.A. *Third Edition.* Extra fcap. 8vo. *cloth*, 2s.

Caesar. The Commentaries (for Schools). With Notes and Maps, &c. By C. E. Moberly, M.A., Assistant Master in Rugby School.
The Gallic War. Second Edition. Extra fcap. 8vo. *cloth*, 4s. 6d.
The Civil War. Extra fcap. 8vo. *cloth*, 3s. 6d.
The Civil War. Book I. *Second Edition.* Extra fcap. 8vo. *cloth*, 2s.

Cicero. Selection of interesting and descriptive passages. With Notes. By Henry Walford, M.A. In Three Parts. *Third Edition.* Ext. fcap. 8vo. *cloth*, 4s. 6d. *Each Part separately, in limp cloth*, 1s. 6d.

Cicero. Select Letters (for Schools). With Notes. By the late C. E. Prichard, M.A., and E. R. Bernard, M.A. Extra fcap. 8vo. *cloth*, 3s.

Cicero. Select Orations (for Schools). With Notes. By J. R. King, M.A. *Second Edition.* Ext. fcap. 8vo. *cloth*, 2s. 6d.

Cornelius Nepos. With Notes, by Oscar Browning, M.A. *Second Edition.* Extra fcap. 8vo. *cloth*, 2s. 6d.

Livy. Selections (for Schools). With Notes and Maps. By H. Lee Warner, M.A. *In Three Parts.* Ext. fcap. 8vo. *cloth*, 1s. 6d. each.

Livy. Books V—VII. By A. R. Cluer, B.A. Extra fcap. 8vo. *cloth*, 3s. 6d.

Ovid. Selections for the use of Schools. With Introductions and Notes, etc. By W. Ramsay, M.A. Edited by G. G. Ramsay, M.A. *Second Edition.* Ext. fcap. 8vo. *cloth*, 5s. 6d.

Pliny. Select Letters (for Schools). With Notes. By the late C. E. Prichard, M.A., and E. R. Bernard, M.A. *Second Edition.* Extra fcap. 8vo. *cloth*, 3s.

Catulli Veronensis Liber. Iterum recognovit, apparatum criticum prolegomena appendices addidit, Robinson Ellis, A.M. 8vo. *cloth*, 16s.

Catullus. A Commentary on Catullus. By Robinson Ellis, M.A. Demy 8vo. *cloth*, 16s.

Catulli Veronensis Carmina Selecta, secundum recognitionem Robinson Ellis, A.M. Extra fcap. 8vo. *cloth*, 3s. 6d.

Cicero de Oratore. With Introduction and Notes. By A. S. Wilkins, M.A., Professor of Latin, Owens College, Manchester.
Book I. Demy 8vo. *cloth*, 6s. Book II. Demy 8vo.*cloth*, 5s.

Cicero's Philippic Orations. With Notes. By J. R. King, M.A. *Second Edition*. Demy 8vo *cloth*, 10s. 6d.

Cicero. Select Letters. With Introductions, Notes, and Appendices. By Albert Watson, M.A. *Third Edition*. Demy 8vo. *cloth*, 18s.

Cicero. Select Letters (Text). By the same Editor. *Second Edition*. Extra fcap. 8vo. *cloth*, 4s.

Cicero pro Cluentio. With Introduction and Notes. By W. Ramsay, M.A. Edited by G. G. Ramsay, M.A., Professor of Humanity, Glasgow. *Second Edition*. Ext. fcap. 8vo. *cloth*, 3s. 6d.

Livy, Book I. By J. R. Seeley, M.A., Regius Professor of Modern History, Cambridge. *Second Edition*. Demy 8vo. *cloth*, 6s.

Horace. With Introductions and Notes. By Edward C. Wickham, M.A., Head Master of Wellington College.
Vol. 1. The Odes, Carmen Seculare, and Epodes. Extra fcap. 8vo. *cloth*, 5s. 6d.

Persius. The Satires. With a Translation and Commentary. By John Conington, M.A. Edited by H. Nettleship, M.A. *Second Edition*. 8vo. *cloth*, 7s. 6d.

Plautus. Trinummus. With Introductions and Notes. For the use of Higher Forms. By C. E. Freeman, M.A., and A. Sloman, M.A. Extra fcap. 8vo. *cloth*, 3s.

Sallust. With Introduction and Notes. By W. W. Capes, M.A. Extra fcap. 8vo. *cloth*, 4s. 6d.

Fragments and Specimens of Early Latin. With Introduction and Notes. By John Wordsworth, M.A. Demy 8vo. *cloth*, 18s.

Tacitus. The Annals. I-VI. With Introduction and Notes. By H. Furneaux, M.A. 8vo. *cloth*, 18s.

Tacitus. The Annals. I-IV. For the use of Schools and Junior Students. By the same Editor. Extra fcap. 8vo. 5s.

Virgil. With Introduction and Notes. By T. L. Papillon, M.A. 2 vols. Crown 8vo. *cloth*, 10s. 6d.
The Text may be had separately, *cloth*, 4s. 6d.

A Manual of Comparative Philology, as applied to the Illustration of Greek and Latin Inflections. By T. L. Papillon, M.A. *Third Edition. Revised and Corrected*. Crown 8vo. *cloth*, 6s.

The Roman Poets of the Augustan Age. *Virgil.* By William Young Sellar, M.A. *New Edition*. 1883. Crown 8vo. 9s.

The Roman Poets of the Republic. By the same Author. Extra fcap. 8vo. *cloth*, 14s.

III. GREEK.

A Greek Primor. By the Right Rev. Charles Wordsworth, D.C.L., Bishop of St. Andrews. *Seventh Edition.* Ext. fcap. 8vo. *cloth.* 1s. 6d.

Greek Verbs, Irregular and Defective. By W. Veitch. *Fourth Edition.* Crown 8vo. *cloth,* 10s. 6d.

The Elements of Greek Accentuation (for Schools). By H. W. Chandler, M.A. Ext. fcap. 8vo. *cloth,* 2s. 6d.

First Greek Reader. By W. G. Rushbrooke, M.L. *Second Edition.* Ext. fcap. 8vo. *cloth,* 2s. 6d.

Second Greek Reader. By A. J. M. Bell, M.A. Extra fcap. 8vo. *cloth,* 3s. 6d.

Fourth Greek Reader; being Specimens of Greek Dialects. By W. W. Merry, M.A. Ext. fcap. 8vo. *cloth,* 4s. 6d.

Fifth Greek Reader. Part I, Selections from Greek Epic and Dramatic Poetry. By E. Abbott, M.A. Ext. fcap. 8vo. *cloth,* 4s. 6d.

The Golden Treasury of Ancient Greek Poetry; with Introductory Notices and Notes. By R. S. Wright, M.A. Ext. fcap. 8vo. *cloth,* 8s. 6d.

A Golden Treasury of Greek Prose. By R. S. Wright, M.A., and J. E. L. Shadwell, M.A. Ext. fcap. 8vo. *cloth,* 4s. 6d.

Aeschylus. Prometheus Bound (for Schools). With Notes. By A. O. Prickard, M.A. *Second Edition.* Ext. fcap. 8vo. *cloth,* 2s.

Aeschylus. Agamemnon. With Introduction and Notes. By Arthur Sidgwick, M.A. *Second Edition.* Ext. fcap. 8vo. *cloth,* 3s.

Aeschylus. Choephoroi. With Introduction and Notes. By Arthur Sidgwick, M A. Extra fcap. 8vo. *cloth,* 3s.

Aristophanes. In Single Plays, edited with English Notes, Introductions, &c. By W. W. Merry, M.A. Extra fcap. 8vo. The Clouds. *Second Edition,* 2s.   The Acharnians, 2s.   The Frogs, 2s.

Cebetis Tabula. With Introduction and Notes by C. S. Jerram, M.A. Ext. fcap. 8vo. *cloth,* 2s. 6d.

Euripides. Alcestis (for Schools). By C. S. Jerram, M.A. Ext. fcap. 8vo. *cloth,* 2s. 6d.

Euripides. Helena. Edited with Introduction, Notes, and Critical Appendix. By the same Editor. Extra fcap. 8vo. *cloth,* 3s.

Euripides. Iphigenia in Tauris. By C. S. Jerram, M.A. *Just ready.*

Herodotus. Selections. With Introduction, Notes, and Map. By W. W. Merry, M.A. Ext. fcap. 8vo. *cloth,* 2s. 6d.

Homer. Odyssey, Books I-XII (for Schools). By W. W. Merry, M.A. *Twenty-Seventh Thousand.* Ext. fcap. 8vo. *cloth,* 4s. 6d.

Homer. Odyssey, Books XIII-XXIV (for Schools). By the same Editor. *Second Edition.* Ext. fcap. 8vo. *cloth,* 5s.

Homer. Iliad. Book I (for Schools). By D. B. Monro, M.A., Provost of Oriel College Oxford. *Second Edition.* Ext. fcap. 8vo. *cloth,* 2s.

Homer. Iliad. Books I-XII. With an Introduction, a Brief Homeric Grammar, and Notes. By D. B. Monro, M.A. Extra fcap. 8vo. *cloth,* 6s.

Homer. Iliad. Books VI and XXI. With Introduction and Notes. By Herbert Hailstone, M.A. Extra fcap. 8vo. *cloth,* 1s. 6d. each.

Lucian. Vera Historia (for Schools). By C. S. Jerram,
M.A. *Second Edition.* Extra fcap. 8vo. *cloth,* 1*s.* 6*d.*

Plato. Selections from the Dialogues [including the whole of the *Apology* and *Crito.*] With Introduction and Notes by J. Purves, M.A. Extra fcap. 8vo. *cloth,* 6*s.* 6*d.*

Sophocles. In Single Plays, with English Notes, &c. By Lewis Campbell, M.A., and Evelyn Abbott, M.A. Extra fcap. 8vo.
Oedipus Rex, Philoctetes. *New and Revised Edition,* 2*s.* each.
Oedipus Coloneus, Antigone, 1*s.* 9*d.* each.
Ajax, Electra, Trachiniae, 2*s.* each.

Sophocles. Oedipus Rex: Dindorf's Text, with Notes by the present Bishop of St. David's. Extra fcap. 8vo. *cloth,* 1*s.* 6*d.*

Theocritus (for Schools). With Notes. By H. Kynaston (late Snow), M.A. *Third Edition.* Ext. fcap. 8vo. *cloth,* 4*s.* 6*d.*

Xenophon. Easy Selections (for Junior Classes). With a Vocabulary, Notes, and Map. By J. S. Phillpotts, B.C.L., and C. S. Jerram, M.A. *Third Edition.* Ext. fcap. 8vo. *cloth,* 3*s.* 6*d.*

Xenophon. Selections (for Schools). With Notes and Maps. By J. S. Phillpotts, B.C.L., Head Master of Bedford School. *Fourth Edition.* Ext. fcap. 8vo. *cloth,* 3*s.* 6*d.*

Xenophon. Anabasis, Book II. With Notes and Map. By C. S. Jerram, M.A. Ext. fcap. 8vo. *cloth,* 2*s.*

Xenophon. Cyropaedia. Books IV, V. With Introduction and Notes. By C. Bigg, D.D. Ext. fcap. 8vo. *cloth,* 2*s.* 6*d.*

Demosthenes and Aeschines. The Orations on the Crown. With Introductory Essays and Notes. By G. A. Simcox, M.A., and W. H. Simcox, M.A. Demy 8vo. *cloth,* 12*s.*

Homer. Odyssey, Books I-XII. Edited with English Notes, Appendices, &c. By W. W. Merry, M.A., and the late James Riddell, M.A. Demy 8vo. *cloth,* 16*s.*

A Grammar of the Homeric Dialect. By D. B. Monro, M.A. Demy 8vo. *cloth,* 10*s.* 6*d.*

Sophocles. With English Notes and Introductions. By Lewis Campbell, M.A. In Two Volumes. 8vo. *each* 16*s.*
Vol. I. Oedipus Tyrannus. Oedipus Coloneus. Antigone. *Second Edition.*
Vol. II. Ajax. Electra. Trachiniae. Philoctetes. Fragments.

Sophocles. The Text of the Seven Plays. By the same Editor. Ext. fcap. 8vo. *cloth,* 4*s.* 6*d.*

A Manual of Greek Historical Inscriptions. By E. L. Hicks, M.A. Demy 8vo. *cloth,* 10*s.* 6*d.*

IV. FRENCH.

An Etymological Dictionary of the French Language, with a Preface on the Principles of French Etymology. By A. Brachet. Translated by G. W. Kitchin, M.A. *Third Edition.* Crown 8vo. *cloth,* 7*s.* 6*d.*

Brachet's Historical Grammar of the French Language. Translated by G. W. Kitchin, M.A. *Fifth Edition.* Ext. fcap. 8vo. *cloth,* 3*s.* 6*d.*

A Short History of French Literature. By George Saintsbury. Crown 8vo. *cloth,* 10*s.* 6*d.*

Specimens of French Literature, from Villon to Hugo.
Selected and arranged by George Saintsbury. Crown 8vo. *cloth*, 9s.

A Primer of French Literature. By George Saintsbury.
Second Edition, with Index. Extra fcap. 8vo. *cloth*, 2s.

Corneille's Horace. Edited, with Introduction and Notes,
by George Saintsbury. Ext. fcap. 8vo. *cloth*, 2s. 6d.

Molière's Les Précieuses Ridicules. Edited with Introduction and Notes. By Andrew Lang, M.A. Ext. fcap. 8vo. 1s. 6d.

Beaumarchais' Le Barbier de Séville. Edited with Introduction and Notes. By Austin Dobson. Ext. fcap. 8vo. 2s. 6d.

Alfred de Musset's On ne badine pas avec l'Amour, *and*
Fantasio. Edited with Introduction and Notes by Walter Herries Pollock.
Ext. fcap. 8vo. *cloth*, 2s.

L'Éloquence de la Chaire et de la Tribune Françaises.
Edited by Paul Blouët, B.A. Vol. 1. Sacred Oratory. Ext. fcap. 8vo. *cloth*, 2s. 6d.

French Classics, Edited by GUSTAVE MASSON, B.A. Univ. Gallic.
Extra fcap. 8vo. cloth, 2s. 6d. each.

Corneille's Cinna, and Molière's Les Femmes Savantes.

Racine's Andromaque, and Corneille's Le Menteur. With
Louis Racine's Life of his Father.

Molière's Les Fourberies de Scapin, and Racine's Athalie.
With Voltaire's Life of Molière.

Regnard's Le Joueur, and Brueys and Palaprat's Le Grondeur.

A Selection of Tales by Modern Writers. *Second Edition.*

Selections from the Correspondence of Madame de Sévigné
and her chief Contemporaries. Intended more especially for Girls' Schools.
By the same Editor. Ext. fcap. 8vo. *cloth*, 3s.

Louis XIV and his Contemporaries; as described in
Extracts from the best Memoirs of the Seventeenth Century. With Notes,
Genealogical Tables, etc. By the same Editor. Extra fcap. 8vo. *cloth*, 2s. 6d.

V. GERMAN.

German Classics, Edited by C. A. BUCHHEIM, *Phil. Doc., Professor
in King's College, London.*

Goethe's Egmont. With a Life of Goethe, &c. *Third
Edition.* Ext. fcap. 8vo. *cloth*, 3s.

Schiller's Wilhelm Tell. With a Life of Schiller; an historical and critical Introduction, Arguments, and a complete Commentary and Map. *Sixth Edition.* Ext. fcap. 8vo. *cloth*, 3s. 6d.

—— **School Edition.** With Map. Extra fcap. 8vo. 2s.

Lessing's Minna von Barnhelm. A Comedy. With a Life
of Lessing, Critical Analysis, Complete Commentary, &c. *Fourth Edition.*
Extra fcap. 8vo. *cloth*, 3s. 6d.

Schiller's Historische Skizzen: Egmonts Leben und Tod,
and Belagerung von Antwerpen. *Second Edition.* Ext. fcap. 8vo. *cloth*, 2s. 6d.

Goethe's Iphigenie auf Tauris. A Drama. With a Critical
Introduction and Notes. *Second Edition.* Ext. fcap. 8vo. *cloth*, 3s.

Lessing's Nathan der Weise. With Introduction, Notes, etc.
Extra fcap. 8vo. *cloth*, 4s. 6d.

Heine's Prosa, being Selections from his Prose Works.
Edited with English Notes, etc. Ext. fcap. 8vo. *cloth*, 4s. 6d.

Modern German Reader. A Graduated Collection of Prose
Extracts from Modern German Writers:—
Part I. With English Notes, a Grammatical Appendix, and a complete Vocabulary. *Third Edition.* Extra fcap. 8vo. *cloth*, 2s. 6d.

LANGE's *German Course.*

The Germans at Home; a Practical Introduction to
German Conversation, with an Appendix containing the Essentials of German Grammar. *Second Edition.* 8vo. *cloth*, 2s. 6d.

The German Manual; a German Grammar, a Reading
Book, and a Handbook of German Conversation. 8vo. *cloth*, 7s 6d.

A Grammar of the German Language. 8vo. *cloth*. 3s. 6d.

German Composition; a Theoretical and Practical Guide
to the Art of Translating English Prose into German. 8vo. *cloth*, 4s. 6d.

Lessing's Laokoon. With Introduction, English Notes, &c.
By A. Hamann, Phil. Doc., M.A. Ext. fcap. 8vo. *cloth*, 4s. 6d.

Wilhelm Tell. By Schiller. Translated into English Verse
by Edward Massie, M.A. Ext. fcap. 8vo. *cloth*, 5s.

VI. MATHEMATICS, &c.

Figures made Easy: a first Arithmetic Book. (Introductory to 'The Scholar's Arithmetic.') By Lewis Hensley, M.A., formerly Fellow of Trinity College, Cambridge. Crown 8vo. *cloth*. 6d.

Answers to the Examples in Figures made Easy.
By the same Author. Crown 8vo. *cloth*. 1s.

The Scholar's Arithmetic. By the same Author. Crown
8vo. *cloth*, 4s. 6d.

The Scholar's Algebra. By the same Author. Crown 8vo.
cloth, 4s. 6d.

Book-keeping. By R. G. C. Hamilton and John Ball.
New and enlarged Edition. Ext. fcap. 8vo. *limp cloth*, 2s.

Acoustics. By W. F. Donkin, M.A., F.R.S., Savilian Professor of Astronomy, Oxford. Crown 8vo. *cloth*, 7s. 6d.

A Treatise on Electricity and Magnetism. By J. Clerk
Maxwell, M.A., F.R.S. A New Edition, edited by W. D. Niven, M.A. 2 vols. Demy 8vo. *cloth*, 1l. 11s. 6d.

An Elementary Treatise on Electricity. By James Clerk
Maxwell, M.A. Edited by William Garnett, M.A. Demy 8vo. *cloth*, 7s. 6d.

A Treatise on Statics. By G. M. Minchin, M.A. *Third Edition.* Vol. I. *Equilibrium of Coplanar Forces.* Demy 8vo. *cloth*, 9s. *Just Published.*

Uniplanar Kinematics of Solids and Fluids. By G. M.
Minchin, M.A., Crown 8vo. *cloth*, 7s. 6d.

Geodesy. By Colonel Alexander Ross Clarke, R.E. Demy
8vo. *cloth*, 12s. 6d.

VII. PHYSICAL SCIENCE.

A Handbook of Descriptive Astronomy. By G. F. Chambers, F.R.A.S. *Third Edition.* Demy 8vo. *cloth*, 28s.

Chemistry for Students. By A. W. Williamson, Phil. Doc., F.R.S., Professor of Chemistry, University College, London. *A new Edition, with Solutions*, 1873. Ext. fcap. 8vo. *cloth*, 8s. 6d.

A Treatise on Heat, with numerous Woodcuts and Diagrams. By Balfour Stewart, LL.D., F.R.S., Professor of Physics, Owens College, Manchester. *Fourth Edition.* Ext. fcap. 8vo. *cloth*, 7s. 6d.

Lessons on Thermodynamics. By R. E. Baynes, M.A. Crown 8vo. *cloth*, 7s. 6d.

Forms of Animal Life. By G. Rolleston, M.D., F.R.S., Linacre Professor of Physiology, Oxford. *A New Edition in the Press.*

Exercises in Practical Chemistry. Vol. I. Elementary Exercises. By A. G. Vernon Harcourt, M.A., and H. G. Madan, M.A. *Third Edition.* Revised by H. G. Madan, M.A. Crown 8vo. *cloth*, 9s.

Tables of Qualitative Analysis. Arranged by H. G. Madan, M.A. Large 4to. *stiff covers*, 4s. 6d.

Geology of Oxford and the Valley of the Thames. By John Phillips, M.A., F.R.S., Professor of Geology, Oxford. 8vo. *cloth*, 1l. 1s.

Crystallography. By M. H. N. Story-Maskelyne, M.A., Professor of Mineralogy, Oxford. *In the Press.*

VIII. HISTORY.

A Constitutional History of England. By W. Stubbs, D.D., Lord Bishop of Chester. *Library Edition.* Three vols demy 8vo. *cloth*, 2l. 8s.
 Also in Three Volumes, Crown 8vo., price 12s. each.

Select Charters and other Illustrations of English Constitutional History from the Earliest Times to the reign of Edward I. By the same Author. *Fourth Edition.* Crown 8vo. *cloth*, 8s. 6d.

A Short History of the Norman Conquest. By E. A. Freeman, M.A. *Second Edition.* Extra fcap. 8vo. *cloth*, 2s. 6d.

Genealogical Tables illustrative of Modern History. By H. B. George, M.A. *Second Edition, Revised and Enlarged.* Small 4to. *cloth*, 12s.

A History of France, down to the year 1793. With numerous Maps, Plans, and Tables. By G. W. Kitchin, D.D., Dean of Winchester. In 3 vols. Crown 8vo. *cloth*, price 10s. 6d. each.

Selections from the Despatches, Treaties, and other Papers of the Marquess Wellesley, K.G., during his Government of India. Edited by S. J. Owen, M.A. 8vo. *cloth*, 1l. 4s.

Selections from the Wellington Despatches. By the same Editor. 8vo. *cloth*, 24s.

A History of the United States of America. By E. J. Payne, M.A., Fellow of University College, Oxford. *In the Press.*

A Manual of Ancient History. By George Rawlinson, M.A., Camden Professor of Ancient History, Oxford. Demy 8vo. *cloth*, 14s.

A History of Greece By E. A. Freeman, M.A., Regius Professor of Modern History, Oxford.

Italy and her Invaders. A.D. 376-476. By T. Hodgkin, Fellow of University College, London. Illustrated with Plates and Maps. 2 vols. demy 8vo. *cloth*, 1*l*. 12*s*.
    Vol. III. The Ostrogothic Invasion. *In the Press.*
    Vol. IV. The Imperial Restoration. *In the Press.*

IX. LAW.

The Elements of Jurisprudence. By Thomas Erskine Holland, D.C.L. *Second Edition.* Demy 8vo. *cloth*, 10*s*. 6*d*.

The Institutes of Justinian, edited as a Recension of the Institutes of Gaius. By the same Editor. *Second Edition.* Extra fcap. 8vo. *cloth*, 5*s*.

Gaii Institutionum Juris Civilis Commentarii Quatuor; or, Elements of Roman Law by Gaius. With a Translation and Commentary By Edward Poste, M.A., Barrister-at-Law. *Second Edition.* 8vo. *cloth*, 18*s*.

Select Titles from the Digest of Justinian. By T. E. Holland, D.C.L., and C. L. Shadwell, B.C.L. Demy 8vo. *cloth*, 14*s*.

Also in separate parts:—
    Part I. Introductory Titles. 2*s*. 6*d*.   Part II. Family Law. 1*s*.
    Part III. Property Law. 2*s*. 6*d*.
    Part IV. Law of Obligations (No. 1). 3*s*. 6*d*.   (No. 2). 4*s*. 6*d*.

Elements of Law considered with reference to Principles of General Jurisprudence. By William Markby, M.A. *Second Edition, with Supplement.* Crown 8vo. *cloth*, 7*s*. 6*d*.

International Law. By W. E. Hall, M.A., Barrister-at-Law. Demy 8vo., *cloth*, 21*s*.

An Introduction to the History of the Law of Real Property, with Original Authorities. By Kenelm E. Digby, M.A. *Third Edition.* Demy 8vo. *cloth*, 10*s*. 6*d*.

Principles of the English Law of Contract, etc. By Sir William R. Anson, Bart., D.C.L. *Third Edition.* Demy 8vo. *cloth*, 10*s*. 6*d*.

X. MENTAL AND MORAL PHILOSOPHY.

Bacon. Novum Organum. Edited, with Introduction, Notes, etc., by T. Fowler, M.A. 1878. 8vo. *cloth*, 14*s*.

Locke's Conduct of the Understanding. Edited, with Introduction, Notes, etc., by T. Fowler, M.A. *Second Edition.* Extra fcap. 8vo. *cloth*, 2*s*.

Selections from Berkeley. With an Introduction and Notes. By A. C. Fraser, LL.D. *Third Edition.* Crown 8vo. *cloth*, 7*s*. 6*d*.

The Elements of Deductive Logic, designed mainly for the use of Junior Students in the Universities. By T. Fowler, M.A. *Eighth Edition*, with a Collection of Examples. Ext. fcap. 8vo. *cloth*, 3*s*. 6*d*.

The Elements of Inductive Logic, designed mainly for the use of Students in the Universities. By the same Author. *Fourth Edition.* Ext. fcap. 8vo. *cloth*, 6*s*.

A Manual of Political Economy, for the use of Schools. By J. E. Thorold Rogers, M.A. *Third Edition.* Ext. fcap. 8vo. *cloth*, 4*s*. 6*d*.

XI. ART, &c.

A Handbook of Pictorial Art. By R. St. J. Tyrwhitt, M.A. *Second Edition.* 8vo. *half morocco,* 18s.

A Treatise on Harmony. By Sir F. A. Gore Ouseley, Bart., M.A., Mus. Doc. *Third Edition.* 4to. *cloth,* 10s.

A Treatise on Counterpoint, Canon, and Fugue, based upon that of Cherubini. By the same Author. *Second Edition.* 4to. *cloth,* 16s.

A Treatise on Musical Form, and General Composition. By the same Author. 4to. *cloth,* 10s.

A Music Primer for Schools. By J. Troutbeck, M.A., and R. F. Dale, M.A., B. Mus. *Second Edition.* Crown 8vo. *cloth,* 1s. 6d.

The Cultivation of the Speaking Voice. By John Hullah. *Second Edition.* Extra fcap. 8vo. *cloth* 2s. 6d.

XII. MISCELLANEOUS.

Text-Book of Botany, Morphological and Physiological. By Dr Julius Sachs. *Second Edition.* Edited, with an Appendix, by Sydney H. Vines. M.A. Royal 8vo. *half morocco,* 1l. 11s. 6d.

Comparative Anatomy of the Vegetative Organs of the Phanerogams and Ferns. By Dr. A. De Bary. Translated and Annotated by F. O. Bower, M.A., and D. H. Scott, M.A. Royal 8vo. *half morocco,* 1l. 2s. 6d.

A System of Physical Education: Theoretical and Practical. By Archibald Maclaren, The Gymnasium, Oxford. Extra fcap. 8vo. *cloth,* 7s. 6d.

An Icelandic Prose Reader, with Notes, Grammar, and Glossary. By Dr. Gudbrand Vigfusson and F. York Powell, M.A. Extra fcap. 8vo. *cloth,* 10s. 6d.

Dante. Selections from the Inferno. With Introduction and Notes. By H. B. Cotterill, B.A. Extra fcap. 8vo. *cloth,* 4s. 6d.

Tasso. La Gerusalemme Liberata. Cantos I. II. By the same Editor. Extra fcap. 8vo. *cloth,* 2s. 6d.

A Treatise on the Use of the Tenses in Hebrew. By S. R. Driver, M.A., Fellow of New College. *New and Enlarged Edition.* Extra fcap. 8vo. *cloth,* 7s. 6d.

Outlines of Textual Criticism applied to the New Testament. By C. E. Hammond, M.A., Fellow and Tutor of Exeter College, Oxford. *Fourth Edition.* Extra fcap. 8vo. *cloth,* 3s. 6d.

A Handbook of Phonetics, including a Popular Exposition of the Principles of Spelling Reform. By Henry Sweet, M.A. Extra fcap 8vo. *cloth,* 4s. 6d.

The Student's Handbook to the University and Colleges of Oxford. *Eighth Edition.* Extra fcap. 8vo. *cloth* 2s. 6d.

The DELEGATES OF THE PRESS *invite suggestions and advice from all persons interested in education; and will be thankful for hints, &c., addressed to the* SECRETARY TO THE DELEGATES, *Clarendon Press, Oxford.*

www.ingramcontent.com/pod-product-compliance
Lightning Source LLC
Chambersburg PA
CBHW020302170426
43202CB00008B/473